Campfire Stories, Volume 3

Campfire Storytelling Series

Campfire Stories

*... **more** things that go bump in the night*
Volume III

edited by
William W. Forgey, M.D.

With special editorial assistance and
original stories
by David R. Scott and Scott E. Power
Illustrations by David L. Sanders

ICS BOOKS MERRILLVILLE, IN

CAMPFIRE STORIES *More Things That Go Bump In The Night*
Copyright 1995 by William W. Forgey, M.D.

Front cover photo copyrighted 1995 by Mikko Lamminpää, Tampere, Finland. This photo was taken during a Finnish scouting campfire program.

Published by:
ICS BOOKS, Inc.
1370 E. 86th Place
Merrillville, IN 46410
800-541-7323

All ICS titles are printed on 50% recycled paper from pre-consumer waste. All sheets are processed without using acid.

Library of Congress Cataloging-in-Publication Data

Scott, David R.
    Campfire Stories : more thimgs that go bump in the night / edited by William W. Forgey : with special editorial assistance and origainal stories by David R. Scott and Scott E. Power.
        p. cm. -- (Campfire storytelling series ; v. 3)
    Summary: A collection of stories about ghosts and other supernatual encounters set in the remote outdoors. Provides advice on storytelling techniques.
    ISBN 1-57034-018-8
    1. Ghost stories, American. 2. Supernatural--Fiction.
3. Storytelling. [1. Ghosts--Fiction. 2. Supernatural--Fiction.
3. Storytelling--Collections. 4. Short stories.] I. Power, Scott E., 1970- . II. Forgey, William W., 1942-   . III. Title.
IV. Series.
PS3569.C6154C36   1995
813'.0873308--dc20   95-44231
                                                        CIP
                                                        AC

6/9 6

TABLE OF CONTENTS

DEDICATION

This book is dedicated with loving memory to our friend Jack - our companion on wilderness trips from Hudson's Bay to Mexico, an adventurer with great courage, wisdom and kindness, and a veteran of many a campfire. His memory will be with us, and the many others who knew him, always.

Thomas A. Todd, Publisher
William W. Forgey, M.D., Editor

DR. FORGEY is Post Advisor, Explorer Post 99, Hobart, Indiana, and a member of the National Committee of Health & Safety, Boy Scouts of America, Irving, Texas. He is also a committee member of the BSA Northern Tier High Adventure Badge, Ely, MN. Dr. Forgey is a Brotherhood Member of The Order of the Arrow, and accomplished his Wood Badge training in 1969.

INTRODUCTION

My first two books of campfire stories were so successful that I naturally turned my attention to a third book. I love to tell stories and that, of course, means that I am always on the lookout for new grist for the story mill. This time I had significant help, but from a most unusual source.

Many years ago, the Director of Natural Resources in Manitoba, Canada, gave me a permit to build a cabin. This cabin was built about 900 miles north of the U.S. border in an area of complete isolation. Since then, approximately 30 youngsters have had the opportunity to spend from three months to a year living in the magnificent wilderness that forms the north of Manitoba.

Two of these young men recently returned from a year-long stay. Naturally, considerable work goes into the preparation for such a trip. Many skills have to be learned, and while most of these deal with woodcraft, medical preparedness and the like, another aspect of the North that one should learn and appreciate is the folklore which that country seems to inspire.

David Scott and Scott Power worked for over a year preparing for their trip. One aspect of living in a cabin for such a long time is the planning of activities. Some of these activities are projects of exploration, some construction of useful items for every day life, but other projects were more cerebral. I asked Dave and Scott to use the inspiration of the cabin experience to help construct a series of short stories that would be suitable for campfire story adaptation.

They learned to travel alone in that wild country, to live for months in the deep bitter cold of winter, and to let their imaginations run wild. The stories in the first part of the book are those which Dave and Scott have told me by a flickering fire.

Stories in the second part of the book include time-honored classics, other great stories, and more tales told by Dave and Scott. Though not specifically inspired by a particular adventure, they are sure to liven up a campfire.

Some of the stories in this book have been written in the first person. For effective campfire story telling, it is generally best to relate a story as if it happened to someone else – in the third person. Thus, the story teller should convert the narrator's character (the first-person character) into someone else, someone who would provide credibility to the event in the tale.

It's also important to outline a story you wish to tell by the campfire. Each of the stories in this book has such an outline, which will remind you of the points that must be made to make the tale complete.

I think that you will enjoy reading and retelling the stories in this book by many a future flickering fire.

–William "Doc" Forgey, M.D.

PART ONE

Stories From The North

These tales were inspired by the authors' adventures at a remote cabin in northern Canada. The stories have a distinctive north-country flavor, and their exotic locales lend to their fireside interest.

DAVE'S PAUGAN

pronounced "pooh gone"

by Scott E. Power

I had never believed in Indian legends until I met Dave, a Catholic priest and missionary from a remote trading post in the wilds of northern Manitoba, Canada, a land where Cree Indian legends prevail.

Dave and I met while I was on a canoe trip into the north. He needed transportation from Neultin Lake back to his post two hundred miles north.

Although I was a safe canoeist, I wondered about my new partner, Dave. But within minutes of our shoving off, he proved to be an accomplished paddler. During conversation he explained that he had lived in the north for five years. He was supposed to leave after one year, but he loved it so much that he insisted on staying. He said that the Indians had taught him a lot, but he still had a lot to learn.

He explained that the Indians had taught him that every human being has a guardian angel called a paugan. The paugan is a protector or spiritual guardian. A paugan will only interfere with reality in extreme life-threatening danger. Typically, a paugan is a likeness of an animal. Each person's paugan is different. One person's paugan might be a cougar, for some an eagle or a wolf, but it is always an animal of significance, of great importance. But there is only one way for a person to discover what type of animal his paugan might be. He must fast and dream for a fortnight, for two full weeks of dedicated misery and deprivation. Only then will the Great Spirit show a person through dreams what his paugan is.

Dave said at first he didn't believe in it. But one day, while he was canoeing with Indian friends north into the barrens to hunt caribou, they found themselves in a wide turbulent river. The water was freezing cold. Even though it was late August, the air temperature was below freezing. Dave and his partner managed to get ashore once they realized how dangerous the stretch of river had become, but the other canoe was blown into the main channel and was being swept into dangerous standing waves. An upset at this point could mean death for the two Indians, but there was nothing that they, or that Dave and his partner, could do to get themselves out of the raging white water. Suddenly there was a swirl under the canoe and to Dave's disbelief an immense moose rose up out of the water and the canoe was lifted upon its back. The moose plunged towards shore and then suddenly sank beneath the waves, but the canoe had been freed from the main current and the Indians were able to desperately paddle their way to shore.

Dave was dazzled with disbelief about what had happened. An Indian called Julyja, a good friend of the minister, explained that the moose was his own paugan and it had saved him once before as a boy. The canoe had been saved by Julyja's paugan.

Well, that was all Dave needed to see. He immediately believed in the reality of the paugan and he wanted to discover his own. He asked Julyja for instruction. Julyja told him to fast for a fortnight, swim naked with the fish, and dream each day. Whatever animal he dreamed about would be his paugan.

The following summer, Dave did all of this faithfully. At the end of his ordeal it was revealed to him that his paugan was a wolverine, one of the most independent and fierce animals of the north country. He had never been saved by his paugan and it had been years since he witnessed it in a dream, but he knew that it existed and that it would watch over him.

I simply could not believe in any of this. Dave told me that my disbelief was wrong. The Cree Indian legend of the paugan was indeed true and if I didn't show respect my safety was questionable.

Several years later, I was making a solo canoe trip on a remote stretch of river in the forest country of northern Saskatchewan. It had been a pleasant trip and I was in no hurry as I was enjoying that beautiful countryside and its occasional sand beaches. The weather had been the best that I had ever had on a northern trip. Perhaps all of this lulled me into a feeling of over-confidence, because a fateful decision caused me to take a chance with a rapids that proved to be a mistake. A rock ripped my canoe open from stem to stern, causing the entire craft to disintegrate in the swirling rapids. My gear had been secured into the boat; perhaps the turbulence of the water tugging on my Duluth packs aided in destroying the canoe. By the time I had swum clear of the rapids, there was nothing to be seen of my canoe or any of my equipment. My initial relief of being alive soon turned to fear. I was hundreds of miles from any help with no food, tent, or extra clothing!

In some ways the first few days were the most difficult. I still had my mosquito netting and some insect repellent, so at least I wasn't eaten alive by the mosquitoes. There was plenty of fresh water to drink. But food – I had none at all. I became more and more miserable during the first several days. I didn't know a person could become so miserable, so hungry. I built myself a shelter and planned to stay in one place, hoping another party might come down the river that summer, or that an Indian trapper or fisherman would come through.

It was just as well that I stayed, for soon the lack of food made me weak. Travel would have been impossible. My repellent ran out and the mosquitoes started adding to my misery by biting through my clothing. My only relief came when I went swimming naked with the fish in the cold stream. Fish that I could never hope to catch.

As the days passed I became strangely tranquil. And while each day become a blur in my memory, there can be no doubt that I was accidentally fulfilling the quest for a paugan. After almost two weeks, a fortnight as Julyja had told Dave, I lapsed into a trance. While in the trance I stared at the clouds above me and I slowly realized that the clouds were forming into a shape. I was lifted out of my daze by the realization that I was going to see my paugan, that it was going to reveal itself to me, that I might be able to appeal to it for safety and deliverance from a certain death in this wilderness.

But the clouds were forming a shape that I was unfamiliar with. It was, naturally, a white blob. The white image seemed to boil and slowly evolved into a strange image that I struggled to recognize. Then it suddenly dawned on me what I was seeing, what my paugan really was. It was not a giant creature after all. Oh, the cloud was large, but my paugan was not. I was staring at a cloud image of a grub!

An insect that lived in rotten trees, that formed a main food source for the mighty bears of the forest, who were so fond of ripping apart dead trees to devour those tasty morsels.

Yes, my salvation lay all around me in the forest. I came out of my trance and grabbed a large rock and easily found a rotten log. I pounded the log apart and revealed a swarm of the maggot-like grubs, scurrying for cover from the daylight. I scooped up entire handfuls of the white bugs and shoved them in my mouth. The bugs squirmed as I crunched them. The taste was surprisingly wonderful. There was, of course, the crunchy sensation as they were squashed between my molars and there was the delightful juice that squirted into my cheeks with every bite. I was delighted at the first taste of food that I had experienced in two weeks.

My life had been saved by my paugan. I could live for weeks, travel for miles, all because I had been saved by my paugan – the white maggot-like grubs hidden all around me in the rotten logs!

STORY OUTLINE

I.   The story narrator tells of meeting Dave, a missionary, who joined him for a canoe trip back to his post in northern Canada.

II.   Dave relates the Cree Indian legend of the paugan, a protective spirit in the form of an animal that everyone has, but the identity of which will only be revealed in a trance that occurs after fasting for two weeks.

III.   Dave sees two Indians rescued from a turbulent river by a moose that suddenly rises from the river, saving their canoe, before disappearing again beneath the waves.

IV.   Dave is told by an Indian to fast for two weeks, swim naked with the fish, and dream each day if he wishes to learn of his paugan.

V.   The narrator does not believe in this legend, but several years later, while on a solo trip in northern Saskatchewan, his boat and all of his possessions are lost in a rapids.

VI.   As he starves he can obtain relief from the mosquitoes only by swimming naked with the fish in the cold water, accidentally fulfilling two of the requirements of the Great Spirit to have the identify of his paugan revealed.

VII.   After two weeks he lapses into a trance, thus fulfilling the last requirement.

VIII.   The paugan is usually a powerful beast, able to protect the owner from dangers of the wilderness. But the narrator's paugan is not a powerful animal, but a grub.

IX.   The lowly grub, a nutritious source of food for many forest creatures, was the only thing that could have saved him from starvation. The narrator had found his paugan and it saved him!

THE LOST PIECE AT BAD CACHE RAPIDS

by David R. Scott

I was waitin' fer one-eyed Mike to come strollin' into my store with his buckskin pouch a' gold dust. He'd always come in 'bout this time ta barter with me fer his winter trappin' supplies. Yet fer some strange reason he was nearly two weeks late. Now a woodsman simply don't worry 'bout a fellow woodsman, but the truth to the matter was that ol' Mike was late and that the river'd soon be froze. To add to the problem I was the only friend Mike ever had; everyone else thought he was a bit off his rocker – after all he did live beyond Bad Cache Rapids. Yet ol' Mike always told me, "If'n ya want the best apple ya gatta risk climbin' out on a limb at the top of the tree." Perhaps it was his risk that prevented him from paddling into town and provoked me into paddling up his way.

The water of the Black Hat River is fairly calm, except fer Bad Cache Rapids. I reckoned it'd take me 12 days to reach the rapids, if'n the weather was in my favor, and an extra four to reach Mike's place. I got Betty the barmaid to watch the store while I was gone. As I paddled on up through the windin' shores I remembered my Granddad tellin' me why the Cree never camped near the rapids.

"Bad medicine, couldn't hear an approachin' enemy if'n ya had the ears of a bull moose!" he used to say. Not to mention the other yarn 'bout the rapids spun by the folks in town, but I put them stories out of my mind.

Finally, in the mid-afternoon on the thirteenth day I could hear the faint drone of the rapids. Now I didn't believe the tall tale told by the town folk, yet fer some reason my fear grew with the building growl of the boilin' water. I paddled my boat a while longer 'till I couldn't paddle no more. I eased the bow of the canoe up onto a sandy bay on the south shore. Snatchin' up my pack baskets I headed upstream to portage, for there was no way I was campin' at or near them rapids. I was halfway up the portage trail when I seen it and I reckon deep down inside a my gut I was expectin' somthin' like this, just didn't want to believe it. Pulled up on the bank was ol' Mike's birch bark canoe an' there wasn't a track around it.

Now everyone knew 'bout the old cabin at Bad Cache, but no one knew whose it was and no one knew of no one who stayed a single night there 'bouts. I made a quick turn and started up the trail towards the old cabin. By now the sun was droppin' in the western sky and some rain clouds was movin' in overhead. Still, despite the conditions, I trudged on up the overgrown trail.

After a while I could see the ol' one-room shack through a green lace of pine needles. The door was hangin' up with one leather hinge (the other one was torn off) so it hung crooked in the door frame. I cautiously peered through the crack expectin' the unexpected.

"Mike.. .you in there?" It was a pretty small cabin so there weren't no use in askin' twice. I stepped on in.

The cabin was, as cabins go, typical for the north country. Scattered cast-iron cookware on the wall, a hand-made table and chair (which was overturned when I got there), one large oil barrel stove, one bunk hangin' from the west wall, and a few rusted traps hung by the door. On the table sat a small oil lamp which I lit, and then I commenced to workin' on the fire. Soon I had the place warm and my belly full a' bannock and moose tongue stew.

After dinner I undid my bed roll and sat on the bunk exhausted from the long day of upstream paddlin'. It was from there that I noticed Mike's pipe in the southwest corner of the cabin. It was a fancy pipe that ol' Mike got from his Granddad and he never went nowhere without it. I stepped across the room and picked it up. The stem of the old pipe had been bitten clean through and it was half full a' half-burnt tobacco. As I put the remainder of the pipe in my pocket, the rain started to come down a bit harder and the rush a' them rapids sounded a bit louder.

Before, I believed ol' Mike to be off in the woods huntin' fer some grub...now I had my doubts. The small oil lamp cast a few dull and broken shadows on the round log walls and the fire could barely be heard over the rain and river. I must admit that at this time I was feelin' my knees a-knockin' and my hands a-shakin'. Nonetheless, because a' that I dropped my pipe whilst I was loadin' it. The pipe gave a jump and then rolled under the low hanging bunk. I leaned my head over the wooden edge to the point where my hair was sweepin' the floor. Against the wall I could make out the bowl of my pipe but I also saw a small box that went unnoticed b'fore. I reached under, nearly fallin' off the bunk, and grabbed the both of 'em. I stared at the ol' box cautiously and finished packin' my pipe. The hinges was rusted and the wood was rottin'. I struck a match and set my tobacco aglow never once takin' my eyes off a' the box. What was inside this dern thing? Gold, WHAT? Fer all I knew it was a human skull, at least that's what the towns folk would tell ya. Maybe it was ol' Mike's skull! I sat there starin' at the box an' draggin' on my pipe for a long while till finally I flung open the lid.

Fortunately there was no human skull, unfortunately there was no gold nor anythin' of the sort. What was in the box made me double up with laughter. It was a child's jigsaw puzzle. Well I knew, bein' as scared as I was, that sleep was out of the question, so I thought I'd try my luck on the puzzle. I was too amused to wonder 'bout its origin so I spread the pieces out on the table and commenced to fixin' it right. On and on I puffed my pipe and worked on placin' the pieces in their correct spots. The roar of the rapids seemed to increase as the rainy night poured on, drownin' out the sound of everything in and outside a' the cabin. After a while of work I had the frame of the puzzle complete and fer some strange reason the puzzle, what I could make out of it, looked familiar. Still I kept on workin' and placin' when suddenly I realized that the puzzle I was workin' on was a picture of the the cabin in which I was holin' up in fer the night. Well, I did find that rather strange, but in lookin' at the good side a' things (at least to ease my fear) it did make the puzzle much easier to fix. On and on I placed the pieces of the puzzle in their correct spots and with each new piece the river grew louder and the lamplight dimmer. Every now and then I would check my backside 'cause if someone (or something) were sneakin' up on me I wouldn't a' heard it (even with the ears of a bull moose). Also, with each new piece, the puzzle became more and more like a picture of the cabin I was in.

I was workin' on the lower right-hand part of the puzzle when I noticed somthin' far too peculiar. That particular part of the puzzle happened to be the northwest corner of the cabin where I had stored my pack baskets and shoot a monkey if my pack baskets weren't in the very puzzle itself! I started to drag on my pipe even though there weren't nothin' in it, still somthin' possessed me to work on that puzzle. Soon I discovered my bedroll, my hat, my leftover stew and then finally myself in this backcountry jig saw. It was almost complete, except fer a few pieces that were missing, which made up the one window at my back. Everything else that was in the puzzle matched the cabin's interior log fer log.

I relit my pipe and studied the puzzle. I checked the box, the floor and the table but the missing pieces weren't nowhere to be found. Leanin' back in my chair I pondered over my situation. The sound of them rapids was now over-powerin' and the lamplight just gave a flicker. Yet in the flickerin' light I found the missing pieces I was a-searchin' fer. Not on the floor and not in the box, but I saw the missing pieces in the puzzle itself. There they were, layin' on the bunk. I was almost too afraid to set my eyes on the old bunk but I had no choice but to do so. I lifted my head up and gazed over the flame of the tiny lamp. Sure enough, there the pieces were on top of my dusty ol' Hudson Bay blanket just waitin' to be dropped into place.

I walked around the corner of the old wooden table and grabbed the pieces in my sweaty hands. Again I sat down at the table and packed my pipe before placin' the pieces into the missing holes. These would make up the windows of the cabin and complete the puzzle. I held my match up to the flame of the lamplight and watched it flood the room with a fiery flash. The smoke from my pipe hung about me like a heavy fog and the river roared on towards town. Finally I picked up the pieces and carefully snapped them into place. At first I didn't believe what I saw, but in the window stood Death itself. It was a figure almost human...but not quite. Its eyes were sunk deep into its skull, its face was wrinkled gaunt and grey, and its hair was long, stringy and smoky white.

It didn't make a sound, just stood there...starin' with a hungry, evil sort a' grin on its face, and if this puzzle was right (as it had already proved to be) this creature was standin' directly behind me. A bead a' sweat dripped down my forehead, causin' my eyes to blink, and then rolled off a' my cheek and splashed onto the puzzle. I couldn't stand the fear no more. I grit my teeth, clinched my fists, an' whirled around in my chair ready and willin' to face anything for the sake a' my life.

Yet the creature was gone! Swallowin' hard, with my eyes wider than a river in the springtime, I let my breath out with a stutter. I looked back at the puzzle, a bit puzzled m'self. There weren't no creature in the puzzle neither, the window in the picture was blank! Had the puzzle lied, was this all just my fear playin' tricks on me?

A cool breeze blew its way through some holes in the wall causing my lamplight to flicker and my spine to tingle. Without a moment to dwell on my questions, the door of the cabin blew off a' its one leather hinge. There before me stood the beast in the window, the thing in the puzzle...there before me stood Death itself.

When it opened the door, it seemed as though the entire river poured into the cabin, the noise from the rapids drowned out my screams of terror. An' there it stood, almost human, but not quite. Its face seemed hollow, its eyes seemed evil and its teeth seemed anxious. It's hair was long grey and stringy and came to rest on its shoulders lying over a buckskin shirt that I recognized as one-eyed Mike's. As a matter a' fact the more deeply I looked at this...this...thing, the more it took to lookin' like ol' Mike. And when it smiled its hollow-toothed smile I knew it was indeed ol' one-eyed Mike himself.

Instantly I grabbed the corner of the table and threw the entire thing on this creature that I had somehow constructed. At nearly the same time, I blasted out a' the door like an eight-legged dog, and ran straight fer the rapids. I couldn't hear it' but I knew that the beast was right behind me. I made it back into town in two days, and four days later ol' Mike made it into town. Not by canoe, and not by horse...but floatin'. His face was mangled, his body scarred and his one good eye and buckskin shirt weren't nowhere to be found. In his mouth was the stem of the pipe that his Granddad had given to him.

The townsfolk have since accused me of bein' a killer, after they found the other half of Mike's pipe in my pocket, and have sentenced me to be the guest of honor at a necktie party. I haven't told them my story for I'd rather face the steps and string than live knowing that creature still lurks in the black spruce forests near Bad Cache Rapids. But the next time one of them towns folk are up that way pannin' or trappin' they'll learn right quick, and you can bet a sack a' gold dust that it'll be my face in that missing window.

STORY OUTLINE

I.   One-eyed Mike is two weeks late returning to town from the mysterious wilderness area called Bad Cache Rapids.

II.   The story teller is about the only friend Mike has, so he takes it upon himself to travel upstream for 12 days to check on Mike.

III.   When he arrives at the Bad Cache Rapids, he finds Mike's canoe, but is unable to locate him at an abandoned cabin.

IV.   He is horrified to find old Mike's pipe as he knew that it was Mike's most prized possession and that he was never without it. He places the broken pipe in his pocket for safekeeping.

V.   When spending the night at the cabin, he finds a small box with a puzzle in it that turns out to be a picture of the cabin's interior, even to include his own pack baskets sitting in a corner.

VI.   Several of the pieces are missing, but upon studying the picture in the puzzle, he notes that they appear on the bed. Sure enough, upon checking the bed there they are.

VII.   When he places the pieces into the puzzle, it shows the window behind him with the figure of Death, appearing as a half-rotten image of his friend Mike, looking in at him.

VIII. He turns around, but the window is empty. Before he can get over this shock, the door blows off the cabin and there stands the creature of death.

IX.   He throws the table at the creature and escapes back to town.

X.   Mike's body soon floats into town, all mangled, but with the pipe stem still clenched in Mike's teeth.

XI.   The town's people arrest, and are going to hang, the story teller as they have found Mike's pipe in his pocket.

XII. The story teller knows that they will not believe his story, but that someday one of them will also go up to that cabin and put the puzzle together, only to see his face in the missing window!

THE NIGHTMARE TRAIL

by Scott E. Power

I considered myself a rational and sensible person until that night. I don't blame anyone for disbelieving me. I often times don't believe it myself, but as soon as I close my eyes to sleep, there it is as vivid as that night. And as horrible.

I'm surprised at myself for trying to explain it all here again. I've told the story many times. Each time people laugh in disbelief. I, too, would laugh if I heard such a story, if it had not happened to me. But it did. I can't deny it. If I hadn't been alone, maybe it wouldn't of happened at all. But I was, it did, and as a result, I will forever shun solitude.

It was the winter solstice, December twenty-first, the longest night of the year. It had been snowing for more than thirty-six hours. For northern Manitoba, the temperature was warm, only ten below zero. The time was around six in the evening. The sun had long since sunken below the horizon as I was snowshoeing to my cabin, returning from my trap line.

Although I was anxious to arrive back at my cabin, which was only a mile down the river, I couldn't help but stop periodically to look around. All I could see through the falling snow was the river bank and jagged tree line, the black spruce stabbing the dark sky with their twisted tree tops. The whole panorama was illuminated by the soft light of the full moon, which was shining behind the thick cover of snow clouds. There was no sound. Only winter's silence literally humming in my ears. I have never understood how, when it is so silent in the north country, there seems to be a distant noise, not unlike the whine of a saw mill.

After a few moments of gazing at what appeared to be an enchanted fantasy land of a child's nightmare, which was really the frozen muskeg of northern Manitoba, I pressed on. The winter's silence was drowned out by the "crunch...crunch...crunch" of the snow beneath my snowshoes.

I was contemplating the epicurean delight of a hot cup of tea back at my cabin when I saw the tracks. They were large tracks, but not the tracks that moose leave behind as they move through snow. They resembled tracks made by a human. But who?

No one lived within fifty miles of my cabin. I didn't remember making the trail. It ran perpendicular to my trap line and to my normal travels. I could not think of a reason why I would have gone that way, unless to satisfy an urge to explore. But the trail was fresh, made within the last few hours. I hadn't seen it earlier while hiking past. Someone, or something, had just travelled through here. If so, they must have seen my trail. What was it? A human? If so, who was it? What were his intentions? Why was he traveling on such a stormy night?

As I pondered these questions, I felt the rhythm of my heartbeat raise to a staccato pounding. The only way to know the answer to this mystery was to follow the trail and find out. If worse came to worse, I had my rifle. But surely this was the trail of a fellow trapper whom I did not know. I turned off my trail and onto the other, following it into the dark gloom of the trees.

I had followed the trail into the woods a hundred yards or so when I began to see dark splotches on the snow. It was a substance I didn't recognize. The splotches were sporadic and of diverse sizes. I took off my gloves to touch them, attempting to identify them by their textures. But of course, the cold temperatures had already frozen the substance into grains of ice.

The thought crossed my mind that possibly blood had dripped from dead game that this unknown person had hunted. I felt comfortable with this thought and ceased to puzzle over it any longer.

I stopped to look over the surroundings. I could no longer see the river behind me. All about me were sinister shadows of gnarled black spruce. Occasionally, I would brush up against a tamarack tree. The cloud cover had begun to thin out and the snow was changing into light flurries. The moonlight was swelling as the clouds dispersed.

The moon itself was full and ominous. The air seemed to be growing colder. I began to feel the frigid air stabbing me like pricking needles through my layers of wool and down. In the distance, I heard the hunger cry of an Arctic wolf.

The trail I followed was longer than I had anticipated and I began to feel as if it went nowhere specific. Just someone, or something, passing through. But that just seemed too outrageous, it had to go somewhere. Much to my surprise, as I continued trekking, I began to recognize various landmarks. I guess you could say I was experiencing a sense of deja vu. I began to feel that I had been there before, but didn't consciously remember it. It was like a dream, or a nightmare.

Finally, just over the sound of the snow crunching beneath my snowshoes, I heard what seemed to be the song of a Canadian Jay. But as I stopped to listen and discern, I realized it was the whistle of a human. At last I was nearing this mysterious person.

As I closed the distance between the whistler and myself, I began recognizing more and more of the surroundings. It was more eerie than bizarre. The hair on my neck stood up as the gloom of the forest was serenaded by someone whistling in the darkness. It seemed to me that I was walking myself into a realm of paradox and surrealism. The atmosphere reeked with the warmth of evil and the frigidity of death. I tried to convince myself to turn around and go home. But not knowing what was ahead, whistling in such a dreadful context, would forever vex me. Besides, I had come this far, and I did have my rifle.

The stains in the snow had become more frequent. I lit a match to examine them more closely. As the match flame illuminated the snow, I saw a dark crimson color. It was definitely blood.

Exactly at that moment, the tune being whistled in the distance changed. At first it had been merry and delightful, however I did not recognize the melody. But now the air was filled with the robust melancholy of Bach's *Toccota and Fugue*. The sound was amplified throughout the forest and resembled a pipe organ more than a whistle. But that was impossible and I knew it. It was all in my head, made worse by my fatigue and terrible imagination.

I looked up from the ground and saw candlelight shining through a cabin window. A cabin! I couldn't believe it. I didn't think there was a cabin within fifty miles of my own. As I approached the cabin stealthily and with great curiosity, I began noticing that the cabin resembled mine. But it was difficult to concentrate and be sure, because the whistle was getting louder. It seemed to weaken me.

I was positive that the cabin looked like my own. The roof was an A-frame, the main cabin was about the same size and there were windows on the east and west walls. And even more peculiar was the fact that the outhouse and woodshed were designed identically to mine.

Suddenly, the person inside stopped whistling. My ears were ringing in its absence. My heart was pounding like a sledgehammer. Although the temperature was below zero, I was sweating. The trail of what I knew to be blood went around the corner of the cabin to the far side, where I assumed the entrance was. Just like mine.

I gazed through the window from where I sat, some twenty yards away, hoping to see who was inside this cabin. Unfortunately, I saw nobody, just a shadow dancing about in graceful glides. I un-lashed my snowshoes, took hold of my gun, and prepared my nerve to go look through the window at the person inside.

As I sat there, I looked down at my hands, which grasped the rifle with a white-knuckled grip, and realized how ridiculous I was behaving. If someone was to have seen me, they would have thought I was a child. I was ashamed. It was mere coincidence that this cabin resembled mine. It couldn't be mine. Besides, what did I think was in there? The windigo? The windigo is part of a Cree Indian legend that embodies all the fear, all the horror, all the wildness, starvation, misery and terrible cold of the North. The windigo is supposedly a man and a cannibal. But it is an Indian legend, not reality. It simply doesn't exist!

I laughed at myself and my imagination. It crossed my mind that I had lived in that God-forsaken-land too long and I was becoming "bushed," as they say in the North. I decided to leave my gun behind and simply go look inside the window to check things out. Then I would knock on the door and introduce myself. Maybe the person would be kind enough to offer me a cup of java. I certainly needed a warm drink. With a huge amount of confidence, I got up from where I sat and walked, as quietly as possible, to the window.

However, as I got closer, my determination began to melt away. I began noticed debris and other objects that I recognized. The spool of rope against the wall. The kerosene barrel. And just a few feet away, I could see a sled that looked like mine. This was my cabin! But how? Who was inside? And why the blood?

Immediately, I grew weak with fright. Everything was too freakish for it to be normal. I felt I had fallen into a trap and there was no way out. I remembered my rifle, but it was to late, I was at the window. I could delay no longer. I had to look in.

I peered in. Everything was as I had left it. But there was a fire burning in the stove, obviously started by this foreigner. And some kind of meet was being fried on the stove. Maybe that was what the blood came from.

I could see the person inside, but not the face. It was a man. He was tall and husky with long white hair. There was something hanging in the corner, but I couldn't tell what it was. The man moved a kerosene lantern onto a table by the stove and I could make out a few more details. It was definitely meat of some sort cooking on the stove. But exactly what kind I couldn't tell. It was still dripping blood and under it was a bucket to catch the fluids. The carcass was hanging from its hind quarters, and the forelegs, minus the severed one, were almost touching the floor. It was a large animal, probably seven feet from tip to tip. The head had been severed.

The man, whose face I still could not see, removed the meat from the stove and, with his back to me, began to eat it. My eyes went back to the carcass. I tried to identify it. I was truly puzzled. Finally, as I let my eyes sweep over the room that was mine, I noticed something next to the lantern. The shadows on it cast from the light were sharp and full of contrast. It was difficult to discern what it was.

I stared and stared until the realization of its identity burned my consciousness with an evil that could only be from hell. My whole body quivered. My heart was overcome with fear. That thing in the shadows of my cabin was a human head! And the carcass was a human body!

I thought I was mad...insane...hallucinating. But there it was. Swinging in the shadows of my cabin. A bloody fresh carcass of a slaughtered human being.

The fear and horror of the evil overcame me. I wanted to run away, but I couldn't move. My whole body was paralyzed and sick.

The cannibalistic man inside stood up from the table where he was eating human flesh, and walked toward the door. He was going outside! I must run! I turned to escape. As I did, I looked up and there he was in front of me! The windigo!

"You're next!" he sneered.

Darkness overcame me. I lost consciousness.

When I awoke, I was inside my cabin. Tucked inside my warm sleeping bag. It was daylight. All was serene.

I looked around. No one was there. He, or it, was gone. Or had he even been there? There was no carcass, no head.

It was all a dream, a nightmare! My terrible ordeal was only a dream.

How good it was to be alive! Really alive! No fear, no horror. All was well.

After breakfast, I had to check my trap line. As I left the cabin, I walked with a bounce, a joy of peace. But as I turned the river bend and approached the spot where my nightmare had started, I slowed with uncertainty. Had it truly been a dream, or not?

Yes! Of course it was a dream. I was still alive wasn't I?

But as I continued trekking, the scar of a freshly made trail perpendicular to mine became visible.

STORY OUTLINE

I.   The narrator finds a mysterious trail leading into the woods, only about a mile from his cabin located in isolated wilderness.

II.   As he follows it he notices drops on the trail that he eventually finds to be blood.

III.   He comes upon an inhabited cabin that he did not know existed.

IV.   Initially scared, his fear increases when he notes that the cabin and its belongings appear to be identical with his.

V.   To his horror, he sees that the body hung in the cabin, and being eaten by its inhabitant, is that of a human being.

VI.   He knows that he has come upon the windigo, the embodiment of all the fear, all the horror, all the wildness, starvation, misery and terrible cold of the North.

VII.   He turns to run from the cabin, but the windigo is behind him suddenly and shouts (and be sure to shout this when telling the story), "You're next!"

VIII. The narrator wakes up, safe in his cabin. It has only been a dream.

IX.   After breakfast he leaves to check his trap line and the story finishes with his noting a freshly made trail, perpendicular to his, just as in the dream.

A TRAPPER'S GREED

by Scott E. Power

Once upon a time, there were two boys who were very good friends. They had many common interests, especially camping. They loved to hike in the woods, set up camp, and spend the night under the stars. The sounds of the night were very alluring and mystifying to them; they really had a great appreciation for the wild in wilderness. Growing up, they had participated in the Boy Scouts and learned much history and technique about camping, canoeing, survival and wilderness first aid. John's grandfather was even a trapper, third generation, and helped teach the boys about the woods and wildlife. He showed them how to live off the land and how to trap for pelts. He taught them everything he knew and they grew up always dreaming of a day when they could go to Grandfather's cabin in northern Canada and live for a winter and trap and learn what it was really like to live off the land and with the land.

Finally, it was high school graduation, and the first real chance the boys had to pursue their dream approached. Upon graduation, Grandfather promised that he would send them to the cabin for a winter to fulfill their dreams if they wanted. They immediately said, "Yes!"

The pre-trip planning went smoothly, time passed quickly, and before the boys knew it the departure date was imminent. These best of friends couldn't wait for the great adventure. It was their dream.

Most of their gear was food, clothing and books. Grandfather had the rest of the essentials already stored at the cabin. Traps, fur stretchers, knives, tools, fishing gear, tents, extra sleeping bags, some nonperishable food, all sorts of things. The friends were all set.

The night before the bush plane was going to fly them into the bush, one of the boys, Ricky, was talking with a local trapper and they discussed many aspects of the job, just like people with things in common will do. When the subject of money came up the old trapper told Ricky that last season that one marten pelt had sold for fifty to seventy dollars – and that the price was expected to stay high for the upcoming season. This news excited both John and Ricky. They didn't realize they could make so much money. It was exciting to think about and they determined to work together and do the best they could to make a lot of money to help offset the cost of their trip. If they could just get fifty pelts each, which was very likely, they would get seven thousand dollars. What a great thing! The friends were elated.

Once the boys got to the cabin in August, everything went well. It was very hard work to get camp up and running, chopping firewood and planning trap lines and everything else that goes into preparing for a long, dark, northern winter.

Finally, the snows of November came and the boys could begin to set up their trap line. Before the trip they agreed to share the line and its maintenance since it was such a tough job, but as they started the line something weird began to happen. John began to act distant from Ricky, almost as if he wished he wasn't there. One night the truth emerged. John told his friend that he wasn't going to share the trap line anymore, that he didn't want to split the money either. He would move downstream and set up his own camp and trap line away from Ricky and his line.

Ricky couldn't believe his ears. This didn't sound like the best friend that he had come to know. John was acting greedy and Ricky was confused about why. He thought they were a team, a partnership, but suddenly John didn't want anything to do with his so-called friend. Ricky was hurt and did his best to convince John to reconsider, but John wouldn't hear it. He was to move downstream a few miles and live through the long, dark, cold winter nights without another person within a hundred miles, aside from Ricky.

At first Ricky hoped that John would get over it. "This is just a phase," he thought. But as the days turned into weeks and the weeks into months, John never recanted or even came to visit. Ricky tried again to reconcile things but John was adamant. He wanted to be left alone. So Ricky finally gave up and left John alone. Meanwhile, Ricky continued with his life and trap lines.

Finally, as spring approached, the trapping ended and each boy had accomplished his goals. Ricky had trapped in the wilderness, living off the land, just as he had always dreamed. His trapping was good, but not as good as John's. Ricky had gathered twenty-five pelts, but John caught sixty. John had worked much harder than Ricky; he really wanted money and at seventy dollars each, sixty pelts would bring in more than four-thousand dollars. In his mind he was gonna be rich, because to him four thousand dollars seemed like a fortune. He was already counting the money and still didn't want to be friends with Ricky. Ricky was hurt, but had come to terms with John's rejection, and accepted it. They had both done the best they could, according to their own goals.

Grandfather arrived at the cabin excited to see how the boys were doing and how successful they had been at living off the land. Upon his arrival he noticed that something was wrong. The boys seemed happy to see Grandfather but didn't really seem very cordial to each other. Grandfather figured something had happened, maybe an argument. Finally, when it was appropriate, Grandfather asked his grandson John confidentially if there was anything wrong between them. John said, "No."

Not satisfied with the answer, Grandfather later asked Ricky if there was anything wrong. Ricky told Grandfather about what had happened. Ricky explained that John hadn't wanted to share the trap lines or the profits, and that they had lived apart for the last six months. He explained that he had tried to reconcile things but John wouldn't agree. Ricky told Grandfather how hurtful it was for him to lose his best friend over the greed for four-thousand dollars. Grandfather was very hurt that his own grandson had missed the point of teamwork, had become greedy, and had ruined a once-cherished friendship.

In John's mind, though, it was worth it. After all, he was going to get at least seventy bucks per pelt and wouldn't have to share it. Yes, he wouldn't have to share his profits. But what John didn't know was that the price for pelts had dropped harshly because there had been a big drop in demand. Grandfather explained the price had been readjusted while they were gone to about five bucks a pelt. John was crushed. He wasn't rich after all. He was a loser. He had let greed and three-hundred dollars destroy what had been a life-long friendship.

STORY OUTLINE

I.   A life-long dream comes true for two boys when John's grandfather sends them to his cabin in the far north to trap and live off the land.

II.   Fur prices are quite high, and John becomes greedy, telling his friend Ricky that he has decided to live and trap alone and not share his catch.

III.   Ricky learns to enjoy the North as best he can, without the friendship of John.

IV.   When John's grandfather comes in to bring the boys home, he notices that something is wrong and finally learns of John's greed.

V.   He then tells John that the fur prices have dropped. John has lived alone all winter and lost his best friend over a mere three-hundred dollars.

CHURCHILL KILLERS

by Scott E. Power

Believe it or not, there is a town in Canada where the law protects one of the most treacherous, fierce, blood-thirsty killers known to man. Not only does the law in this town protect the killer, but allows it the freedom to walk the streets, mingling with the citizens. Of course, the citizens hate this and do everything in their power not to associate with the killer and even carry guns to protect themselves.

But this killer is protected by law, and if anyone was to kill it there would be a full investigation as to the nature of the killing, to find out if it was done in self-defense. That would be the only justifiable way to kill the killer.

A cab driver in this town was involved in such an investigation. He did what many of the townsfolk wished they could. He murdered the killer.

It was late on a Thursday night and the sky was speckled with stars.The air was cool, but not cold. Perfect walking weather, which is exactly why Ross refused a ride home from one of his friends and insisted on walking home.

For Ross it was in most ways a typical Thursday night. He had just gotten off work and met a few close friends at a town bar for a drink and a game of pool. But on this night Ross became abnormally tired and decided to leave early and go home to sleep. One of his buddies immediately offered him a ride home, but Ross refused, saying the cool night air would do him good. Besides, he only lived a few blocks away. Ross would never again refuse a ride home.

The walk home was as splendid as Ross had hoped. Instead of taking the shortcut through the park, he walked a longer route so he could enjoy the brilliance of the stars and the crisp air.

As he approached his house he could feel the breeze blowing off Hudson's Bay. It was getting chilly and he thought to himself that he was glad to be almost home and close to his warm bed. Turning the corner, he could see the eight steps leading from the sidewalk to his porch. By now he was very fatigued and joked with himself about not being able to climb the steps. But he did, and as he climbed each one, he looked down so as not to stumble. At the same time he fumbled for his house key, which had settled deep down in his pocket.

Finally, at the top of the stairs and on his porch, he walked toward the door which was inside a foyer. He noticed the porch light had burned out and grumbled about how difficult it was to see. Then, he realized the door was gone. In the darkness he stepped on broken glass and splinters of wood, and knew the door had been destroyed.

Then, all at once, it happened. The reality of his worst nightmare was upon him in the darkness. He could sense it. Feel it. But there was nothing for him to do except look up and face it. For in the darkness of his porch he could see the outline of the thing he had feared all his life. The thing that had made his town of Churchill, Manitoba, so popular, yet so deadly. For in the blackness where he stood was the killer, a polar bear.

To understand the horror Ross was facing, you must realize that polar bears, an endangered species protected by law, are the only mammals with no natural predators. They are the King of Beasts and fear nothing. They stalk and kill humans. Without the power of a shotgun, you are helpless. You die by the ripping teeth and crushing jaws of the white bear beast. It will kill you and eat you.

Ross knew this. Ross didn't have a shotgun. Although bears can out-run humans, Ross had no other choice but to run. And he did. Ross ran and ran and ran. He did not look back. But he could hear his predator growling and grunting as it chased its prey.

Ross saw in the distance his only hope, the church. Often in the small community of Churchill, the church doors were left opened for its members and, if that held true this night, he had a chance to live. Panting and sweating, with his heart hammering inside his chest cavity, he reached the church doors, clutched the door handle with a white-knuckled grip and pulled. It was locked.

At this moment, he looked to his right and saw his killer running straight for him. The bear was so close he could hear the gravel crunching underneath its huge paws.

Ross took off running again – this time for the bar where he knew the door would be open and his friends would be inside. It was his last hope.

As he ran he was able to make quick turns between buildings and through an alley that gave him a few seconds more of a lead on the bear. Finally, the tavern was in sight and the lights were on inside. His friends were still there!

He got to the door and could hear laughter inside. There was no time to think, his killer was closing in. Ross put his right hand on the door handle and put his left hand on the oblong window parallel to the door. He pulled the handle with so much force his left hand went through the window shattering it and cutting his hand to shreds. The door was locked! He couldn't reach far enough through the window to open it from the inside. He knew it was over. He turned around to see the bear closing in. He stood there awaiting his death.

But as Ross stood there in shock, a taxi cab turned the corner onto the street. The driver saw the bear closing in on the motionless man in the tavern doorway. The animal had crossed the road and was just feet away from Ross. Knowing he had no time and no alternatives, the driver slammed the accelerator to the floor. The taxi flew over the curb toward man and bear at more than fifty miles per hour.

The car hit the bear, destroying both the auto and the beast – all not more than ten feet from where Ross stood!

STORY OUTLINE

I.   Ross walks home late one night from a bar where he had been drinking with some friends.

II.   When he arrives at his porch he sees a huge polar bear on his step.

III.   All he can do is turn and run. The bear chases him.

IV.   Ross runs through the little town of Churchill and tries to find shelter inside buildings, but all the doors are locked. The bear is closing in.

V.   He arrives back at a bar and tries the door, but it is also locked. There is no other place to run. He turns around and watches the bear running toward him, ready to eat him alive.

VI.   As Ross stands preparing to die, a taxi cab turns the corner and the driver sees what's happening. The driver speeds up and deliberately hits the bear, killing it, totaling the car and saving Ross's life.

A KNOCK AT THE DOOR

By David R. Scott

Editor's Note: In this story, Dave almost seems to be getting even with me for sending him to the cabin. At least, he puts a character with my background into a horrible predicament.

Long ago, I built a small log cabin in the northeastern corner of Manitoba, Canada. Every so often, I find two youngsters willing to capture the experience of a lifetime by living there for an extended period of time. I help them finance the expedition and they in turn pay me back by living out an adventure that I could not experience myself. The cabin is located 200 miles from the nearest town and at some points on the compass a thousand miles away from the nearest human. It is only accessible by bush plane. Once a crew is in the bush, I usually fly in once every four months to resupply them and to make sure they are in good health. (It is also a good excuse for me to escape to the cabin I love.)

I had sent two young men up for a one-year expedition and I had checked on them twice. It was now nearing Christmas time and I was on my way to take them out of the bush and back into the "civilized world." It was a trip that I had looked forward to with great anticipation, however it resulted in my worst nightmare.

The sound of the single-engine Beaver rang in my ears as I watched the Land of the Little Sticks pass beneath its skis. The temperature had plummeted to forty below that day and the thought of a hot cup of coffee and a toasty log cabin warmed my soul. I had so much to tell those guys about the world they had left behind. My heart began to pound in my throat when I saw the mighty Churchill River, I knew I was getting closer. It had always been such an exciting moment to fly low over the cabin and see two weathered woodsmen come running out with their faces full of smiles and their arms waving. Exciting, indeed, and relieving, for I knew at that moment they were alive and well. The thought of no one coming out of the cabin scared me more than anything, but it was the chance one took, and I had great faith in the crews I had sent up in the past.

Soon we were flying over the Smith River, and in the distance I could see the bend on which the cabin was located. I pointed it out to the pilot and he aimed the nose of the plane straight for the cabin, but something was wrong. No smoke was visible from the cabin's stove pipe. As we drew nearer my nightmare became a reality. Not a single sign of life was present. No tracks to the river, no smoke from the pipe, no firewood cuttings...nothing. I had the pilot buzz the cabin as low as he could. No one came out! The pounding of my heart increased with every beat. We flew up to the drop-off point one mile upstream and the pilot gently brought the plane down.

"I can't wait for ya or the engines'll freeze up. Do ya wanna stay 'r go?"

"Pick us up in one week." I replied. I used "us" simply because I refused to believe anything had gone wrong. I pulled my gear up onto the bank and watched the airplane disappear into the empty Arctic sky.

Quickly, I strapped on my snowshoes and headed downstream toward the cabin, stumbling from time to time, intoxicated with fear. Finally, through the dense black spruce I could make out the roof of the cabin. To my ears my footsteps were silent, and the wind, though blowing briskly, made no sound. All I could hear was the beating of my heart.

There was no sign of life whatsoever...none! The front door of the cabin was wide open. I stepped in, and struck a wooden match upon the surface of the cast-iron stove top. The room flooded with a fiery flash and when my sight returned from a state of temporary blindness, I lit a small kerosene lamp.

Through the dim lamplight I could see both chairs were overturned, pots and pans were strewn about the floor, the stove pipe was disconnected and the ladder to the sleeping loft was broken. I picked up the one chair and placed it by the small table. After starting a fire I sat by the stove in a state of shock, I assumed I had lost two very good friends. It was from this point that I noticed Scott's closed journal on the floor along with some other fallen books. In haste and desperation I grabbed the journal and began to read, hoping to find some clues. It read:

Oct. 15, 1991

"I awakened in the middle of the night last night for reasons unknown. I was having a difficult time falling back asleep when I first heard it. There was a knock at the door. Three times in a slow steady progression. I knew that it couldn't possibly be a human for there is no one within 200 miles of here. I awakened Dave to see if he had heard anything, yet he had heard nothing. Perhaps it was a figment of my rather creative imagination, but I could have sworn that I did indeed hear a knock at the door."

He continued on with the day's events and weather documentation, but said nothing more about the knock until two days later.

Oct. 17, 1991

"Well, Dave and I are in the loft right now. Dave is almost asleep and I am catching up on my journal entries. The day has been great. Got a lot of firewood cut and started building a new table beneath the east window. Also went hunting and got a few ptarmigan so dinner was exceptionally good tonight. Dave and I are going to head up to...I just heard that knock again. Dave didn't believe me when I told him I heard it two nights ago, but now he hears it too."

I flipped the next pages but there was nothing more to be read – that was Scott's last journal entry. Jumping up from my chair I began searching for Dave's journal, tearing the cabin apart as I looked. After a great deal of difficulty I found it up in the loft. The journal was wrinkled and appeared as though it had been through a battle. I found it face down, opened to the date Oct. 19, 1991. I read even though the writing was shaky and nearly illegible.

Oct. 19,1991

"Scott has not returned since the night before last. He offered to check out the knock since I was nearly asleep. He went downstairs with the gun, opened the door, but never came back. There was no sound, no scream, no nothing; it was almost as if he was swallowed by the night in the black spruce forest. I spent all of yesterday and part of today searching for him, but have not found so much as a clue. I am in the loft right now. It is in the middle of the afternoon and I did not sleep last night because I, too, heard the knock. Three knocks in a slow steady progression, just as Scott and I had heard the night before last. I am afraid and alone. My partner is gone and I have no choice but to stay here for two and a half more months, to stay here with whatever has been haunting us. I am going outside to try to find whatever it was that did this. I just pray that I am back to document the events tomorrow. If there is no more writing in this journal from this point, then my advice to you (whomever you may be) is to get the hell out of here as fast as you can. Chances are you'd be better off if you were..."

That was it, the rest of the journal was blank, Dave had never finished what he was attempting to write. I leaned my head against the wall, and in the dim lamplight I saw eight scratches running down the floorboards. I also saw a loaded rifle with the hammer back in the far corner of the loft. Whatever had been knocking on the door didn't wait for Dave to finish his journal entry, nor did it wait for him to come outside. Instead, it came and got him, dragging him and causing him to claw the very floorboards in an attempt to escape and save his own life!

My fear intensified. The thought of those guys having been killed was devastating, and the thought of what killed them was even more terrifying. Yet, I was also on the menu...I could feel it. By then the sun had set. I couldn't eat anything for I was nauseous. Instead I loaded my rifle and sat in the loft, too terrified to move. The night dragged on. Eventually my fire burned out, yet I didn't risk going downstairs to feed it. I simply sat shivering in my sleeping bag waiting for the dark night to fade into day.

Morning came with the singing of whiskey jacks and the fighting of martens. The sky was clear and the temperature cold. Soon, I had the fire going and coffee boiling on the buckled top of the old wood-burning stove. I was still in somewhat of a state of shock, so I didn't even notice the coffee boiling over. Quickly I grabbed the pot off the stove, and with shaking hands poured myself a cup.

The day progressed as slowly as the night and my fear grew with each passing moment I was there. I spent the day cutting firewood and reopening an ice hole, always looking for clues and always looking over my shoulder. Soon darkness fell upon the Arctic land and once again I sat in the loft of my cabin awake with a fearful anticipation of the night. My eyes were wide, my knuckles were white, and my finger remained poised on the trigger.

Suddenly, without warning, something jumped in the far corner of the loft, and before I knew it, the rifle was jumping in my hands, emitting spears of sparks and splintering the roof logs with each and every shot. When the smoke cleared, I saw the culprit, although I hardly believed it possible for such a creature to kill two grown men. What I'd believed to be a horrid beast was nothing more than a small squirrel seeking the warmth and comfort of my cabin. Instead, he received six rounds from a lever-action .30-.30. He now was a permanent part of the cabin's floor.

"Let that be a lesson to ya," I shouted beyond the walls of the cabin and into the empty black forest. "Anything that moves within my sight will die within my sight as well...so help me God!" Outside the wind took a deep breath, causing the tree limbs to release their grip on the snow to which they so desperately clung. The wind lazily exhaled in a way that made me realize that my fear was of no importance to her. Whether I lived or died was far from her concern. After all, this was big country, and up here there are no corners in which to back into. A man can run...but he cannot hide.

The next four days followed the same pattern, and each day my fear grew to the point where I was too terrified to accomplish anything. Each new sound that echoed from the black spruce forest provoked a fear in me that I can not explain. Each new night became a gamble, a game of Russian Roulette. I never knew on which night I would hear the knock at my door. I never knew if I would live to see the light of tomorrow.

Finally, it was my last night in the cabin. Tomorrow the bush plane would come to take me out of my nightmare. I climbed into the loft of the cabin and zipped myself into my sleeping bag, laying the gun over my lap. I remembered giving the boys a quote by the famous woodsman Calvin Rutstrum, who said, "An absolute wilderness is a place where you can yell your head off for help and no one will hear you!" I knew I was in such a place. I was defenseless, helpless and completely on my own. Never before have I felt a fear such as that.

Outside the winds rose and fell as if the night were breathing once again. My eyelids became heavy and I could no longer fight the sleep that I had been avoiding for the past week. For the first time since my arrival, I was in a deep sleep. Thoughts of the bush plane filled me with hope.

Morning came bright and cold, I started the fire and set the coffee to boil. I was overwhelmed knowing that the bush plane would be arriving today to take me out of the bush, and out of this living hell. I was preparing to fry some back bacon when suddenly there came a knock at my door...three times in a slow steady progression ...knock...knock...knock!

I bolted upright in my sleeping bag, clutching my rifle and sweating profusely. Morning had been a dream. It took me several minutes to catch my breath and to release the white-knuckled grip I had on my gun. I must have been asleep quite some time, for I noticed that the moon was nearly set in the western horizon. I laid down again and closed my eyes, listening as my own heart pounded the rhythm of absolute fear. I was between the stage of being asleep and awake when I heard it...three times in a slow steady progression, just as the journals had said, yet this time it was no dream. Knock...knock...knock!

My throat went dry, and my knuckles went white around the stock and grip of my gun. The noise didn't recur for several minutes and then it repeated. Knock...knock...knock!

I sat in silence for an eternity. My back was wedged up against the wall and my gunbarrel was aimed at the top of the ladder leading up to the loft. Even in the freezing temperatures my face was beaded with sweat. I didn't move from that spot for the rest of the night. Nothing else happened.

I watched the sun come up through the tops of the spruce trees. Its beams of light came through the frosted windows, illuminating the cabin with a cold light. Quickly, I packed my bags along with the boys' journals and headed for the drop-off point. I recalled the pilot telling me that he'd be there in the early afternoon, and that I should be ready and waiting. I was ready to say the least.

I arrived at the drop-off point at 1 P.M. My ears strained for the sound of a bush plane. The wind was calm and the land stood still. Anxiously I panned the sky for my ride home. Was it getting late or was I paranoid, where was my flight?

Finally in the cool, clean air I could hear the drone of the engines getting closer and closer. The sound, however, demonstrated the Doppler effect, roaring overhead and then onward toward Churchill. Two more hours I waited, yet my plane never showed.

It had happened before in the past, but this was a time of desperation and due to the fact that my pilot was a freelance flyer no one else would know where I was. I hiked back to the cabin for another night of indescribable fear. I arrived at the cabin past dusk. The sky was on fire with vibrant reds and oranges. I relit the stove and set some coffee to boil on the stove top. I also lit all of the lanterns and began to read, trying to fool myself into believing that I was no longer afraid. Eventually I climbed into the loft with my gun and extra shells. I could hear the wind licking the treetops and my heart pounding with fearful anticipation. Once again I wedged myself into the corner of the loft, poised with the gun ready to kill anything that moved.

My fearful anticipation was short-lived. Two hours after I had climbed into the loft I heard the knock, three times in a slow steady fashion. Knock...knock...knock. I held the rifle to my chest and closed my eyes, hoping that this thing would go away as it had done before...but it didn't. Instead I heard the hinges of the cabin's front door slowly squeak as it opened, and then, for a brief moment, they paused, and then they squeaked once more until the door met the wall. The front door was now wide open, and the creature was in my cabin. I jumped up screaming in utter terror for my life and began firing through the floorboards at whatever was beneath me. Finally, I heard the old wooden door creak upon its rusty hinges until it was shut. The creature escaped, and from the sound of its patient exit, it escaped unharmed. My fear increased in its intensity. I was too afraid to go below so I hid in my sleeping bag overcome by exhaustion.

I awoke the following morning still immersed in fear. For three hours I sat deaf to all sounds, blind to all sights and numb to all feeling. It was almost as if someone had shut down all of my senses.

The only thing I do remember was finally snapping out of my state of unconsciousness. I turned my fear into rage. I was angry because this "thing" hadn't put me out of my misery the night before. It was almost as if it fed off my fear, as if it could taste it, as if it enjoyed it. I reloaded my gun and climbed down the ladder. The moment my feet hit the un-level wooden floorboards, there came a knock at the front door three times in a slow steady progression. Knock...knock...knock.

A rush of adrenaline overpowered me and without second thought, I opened fire on the front door. Six shots I fired from the hip, screaming wildly as I pulled the trigger. When the smoke cleared, I heard the thing drop heavily to the ground.

Quickly, I reloaded my gun and stepped up to the door. I took one deep breath, pulled the hammer back on the rifle, and kicked open the door. There, in the crimson snow lay the bush pilot with blood pouring profusely from six large holes in his chest. His face displayed the struggle of his final breath and his eyes were opened wide with shock. It was at that moment I realized that I had just condemned myself to a life sentence in a living nightmare. Off in the distance I heard a laugh echo throughout the black spruce forest, and soon after, the sun fell into the gaping jaws of the horizon.

STORY OUTLINE

I.   The narrator visits a cabin in the far North where he had arranged for two young men to spend the winter.

II.   When flying over the cabin, he sees no sign of human life, and discovers when he lands that the boys have been missing for some time.

III.   In the cabin, he uncovers one of the boy's journals and find out through reading its last entry that someone or something was knocking at the cabin door.

IV.   He discovers through reading the second boy's journal that the other boy had vanished. The second boy never made another journal entry either.

V.   All that week, he lives in absolute fear, for he does not know if or when the knock will sound at the door. Finally, the night before the plane is to arrive, there comes a knock at the door, but the thing goes away.

VI.   The next morning, he leaves to meet the plane. But the plane never comes. Scared beyond belief, he is forced to spend another night in the cabin.

VII.   Very late that night, he hears the knock but this time the creature comes inside the cabin. In blind terror, he begins shooting down through the floorboards of the loft at the creature, and when he finishes firing, he hears the door slowly close.

VIII. The next morning, he is at first paralyzed with fear, then angry. When there are three knocks at the door, he fires all six rounds from the shotgun into the door, and hears the creature drop dead outside in the snow.

XI.   He kicks open the door only to find the bush pilot with six holes in his chest, dead in the white snow. he has just signed and sealed his reservation in a living nightmare.

DREAM OF PAIN

By Scott E. Power

John had been living at a remote cabin in the north, outside a small Indian fish camp, for more than ten months. His time was spent trapping and exploring, and he had been very successful with each. His trap line had yielded many pelts, and his explorations had led him into majestic landscapes. He felt that life in the wild, free from modern-day conveniences and technology, was well-worth the price of solitude he had to pay. Besides, he liked being alone, able to do what he wanted when he wanted, without schedules and clocks.

John enjoyed living near the Indian camp. The Indians were his friends and many hours had been spent in fellowship and fun. He had learned much from the Indians; how to track animals for hunting and trapping, how to live off the land with minimal impact. But there was one thing that John had not learned from the Indians yet; the importance of dreams. Not because the Indians had not tried to teach him – they had tried many times to make him aware of the prophetic nature of the dream world. John simply was unconvinced that dreams were anything more than coincidental. No matter how hard the Indians tried, John would simply laugh at their teachings, saying he was too much of a white man to believe dreams had any reality. But one day the Indian chief came to John with an urgent message. John could see the anxiety on the chief's face and was greatly concerned.

"What's the matter, chief?" asked John.

Without hesitation the chief began to explain. "John, the dream world has spoken to me. The prophecy came to me last night as I slept. My people and I are moving our camp north, away from this place. It is cursed and if we do not move we shall perish. The pain of death is upon this place and I feel it strongly even now as I speak to you. We shall leave tomorrow. I will miss you John."

"Nonsense," John replied, "Chief, it was just a nightmare. That is all. This place is as beautiful as any and plentiful with game. I feel that if you move you shall be mistaken. Please, I beg of you, don't relish your dreams as prophecy. If so, they will keep you running forever. Stay here near the camp and we shall enjoy a prosperous winter."

"That is your problem, John. You have learned our ways and understand our methods very well. But you have failed to respect and live by the lessons of one's dreams as we do. You must correct this, lest it be your downfall. I urge you to come with us and leave this place of pain and death," the chief begged.

"I'm sorry chief, but you must live by your ways and I must live by mine. I shall stay. I wish you well and my love goes with you. Please proceed safely. I will think of you often," John said.

"Not as often as I shall think of you, John," answered the chief.

The two men hugged and the chief departed. It took awhile for John to get used to the absence of his Indian friends. When he would pass the deserted camp he wondered about them. He was sorry that they held their dreams so valuable. He could not understand why or how they would let such nonsense dictate their actions.

The Indians had been gone thirteen weeks when one day while John was hiking back to the cabin, carrying fresh meat just killed for dinner, he began to experience a slight toothache. When he got to the cabin he took a couple of his remaining aspirin for the pain. He was glad he had brought them. He thought for sure he had plenty.

The aspirin did such a good job of stopping the pain, John forgot all about the toothache. That night, however, he was awakened by the same toothache. The aspirin had worn off. He lit a kerosene lantern, and made his way to the bottle of aspirin. He took two more pills and went back to bed.

After a few moments of tossing and turning, John fell asleep again. During his rest, he began to dream. In his dream, he saw himself in the corner of the cabin, curled up on the floor holding the rifle. He was crying and screaming something. But, as in most nightmares, he couldn't hear what he was saying.

In the morning when he awoke, John was a bit disturbed by the dream. Although he didn't think the dream actually meant anything, he still wondered what caused such a vision. Why would he be lying in the corner of the cabin, holding the rifle and crying? He hadn't cried in years, and typically did not hang out in the corners of the cabin. Oh well, it was just a dream, nonsense. It didn't mean anything.

As the morning wore on, John's tooth starting throbbing again which made him forget about the dream. He took more aspirin, but this time he took three tablets, because the pain was a more extreme. Once again, the pain left as the medicine took affect.

John counted the number of aspirin he had left: fifty. He was pleased there were so many. He was certain the tooth ache would eventually subside. He was confident there would be no need for many more aspirin. He was wrong.

As the daylight of winter became less and less, the pain from John's cavity grew and grew. He didn't have a mirror to examine the decayed area, but with his tongue he could feel a gaping hole in one of his molars. Each day John took more and more aspirin, till eventually he only had three left. He couldn't sleep through one night without waking up from the pain. Or the nightmare.

As the pain of the toothache got worse, the horror of John's dream intensified. And the dream had become more confusing. The pain of his cavity seemed to increase as the dream wore on. Eventually, John suspected the dream somehow made the pain worse. But that was ridiculous; he was starting to sound like his old Indian friend.

After each episode of the nightmare, John would wake up in a agonizing and painful sweat. Finally, the three remaining aspirin were gone. John had no more pain-killing chemicals, but lots of pain. No longer could he sleep or do anything without feeling as if his face was being smashed by a lead pipe. Eventually he couldn't even walk without it somehow increasing the pain. His face and gums had become grotesquely swollen.

Getting drunk became John's only way of subduing the pain enough to eat or sleep. He would drink three double shots of whiskey to ease the pain superficially. It would take three times that to give any long-term relief. But of course, John only had so much booze. It wasn't too long before he ran out of that too.

His saving grace was his friend Gavin, a bush pilot. Every long winter month, give or take a week or two, Gavin would stop by via helicopter to drop off supplies. This had been prearranged before John had actually gotten to the cabin. After spring break-up, John was planning to leave the cabin to bring his winter catch of pelts back to civilization. But he hadn't even been able to check his traps. The severe pain of his cavity had really immobilized him. He was now limited to laying down with little movement, except that which was absolutely necessary.

As John laid there day after day, he hoped and prayed for Gavin's arrival. John knew Gavin would bring additional drugs and booze, but more important, he would be able to leave with Gavin, go back to civilization and have a dentist extract the tooth.

John caressed his face with his rough, dirty hands. The corroding tooth was still causing his left cheek to be swollen with pain. He didn't dare touch it with any pressure, the pain was much too intense. At times John cried like a baby because of the suffering. He wished he had heeded the advice of his friend the chief, but it was too late. He had never known such pain in all his life. All he could think about was Gavin's arrival. John knew that it could be one day or one week until he arrived. Not knowing was torture. In the past Gavin had come days early and days late. So much was determined by the weather, there was no way to know for sure. He knew he must hold on and persevere.

Somehow despite the pain, John was able to fall asleep. As it had been every night, he began to dream and his nightmare played once again. He saw himself lying on the floor, gun in hand, crying like a baby. But this time the dream ended differently. Usually John would wake up from the pain of his cavity, but this time he woke up not from the pain, but because of a loud crashing noise.

Opening his eyes quickly, he wondered what the commotion was all about. Lifting his head slowly, trying to ignore the pain, he looked around. There were pots and pans on the floor everywhere. Something had knocked them all down. A wolverine! A wolverine was in the cabin. Momentarily forgetting his condition, John quickly grabbed the rifle and drew down on the beast.

At this time two things happened. The first thing was that as John moved about, he scared the wolverine and it escaped from the cabin.

The second thing was destiny. As John stood watching the wolverine escape, a surge of throbbing pain raped his mouth, sending him into a paroxysm. The interior of the cabin began to fade from his sight as the scene blackened. John fainted and fell to the floor. Moments later he regained consciousness. After he awoke, John wasn't sure if what he saw was reality or his nightmare again. Regaining his thoughts, he tried to remember what had happened. Thinking was difficult but vaguely he remembered the wolverine. Although the pain was consuming, he tried to understand his situation.

He had fallen to the cabin floor, and was lying in the corner, holding the rifle. It was the scene he had witnessed night after night after night. He began to realize the reality of his dream and its prophetic nature. Tears began to stream down his bloated cheeks. He wanted to go back in time and leave with the Indians, or cry out for the chief and his wisdom, but it was far too late for that. The dream was a vision, a prophecy. He could bear the pain no longer and knew what had to be done. He would have to use the gun and relieve the pain.

Gavin could be days longer in arriving and John couldn't last. The pain was causing him to lose consciousness. John had no more pain pills or booze. He never knew pain could be so real, so overwhelming, consuming, destructive. Yes, he would have to kill the pain.

Crying both from the reality of his suffering and imminent death, John placed the barrel of the rifle underneath his jaw. Closing his eyes, wishing there could be another way, he squeezed the trigger.

POOOOOOOOOOOWWWWW!

Instantly, the pain was gone.

STORY OUTLINE

I.   John is warned by an Indian chief to respect dreams and their prophetic nature lest it be his downfall.

II.   The Indian is warned by a dream to move the Indian settlement.

III.   After the Indians have been gone for awhile, John begins to experience a toothache and a recurring dream.

IV.   Eventually, the toothache gets so bad that John uses all his aspirin and booze as pain killers.

V.   John realizes that his nightmare had been a prophecy.

VI.   To escape the pain, he kills himself.

THE PICK-UP

By Scott E. Power

For Hap it was just another day in the sky. A bush pilot in Northern Canada for twenty-three years, Hap barely had to think about flying. After so many years, he knew planes and the art of aviation as well as he knew his own name. Hap had even flown aeronautical stunts for the silver screen.

With skin that looked like tanned leather, a person could see experience in Hap's face. Once, he had hair. Now, he was almost bald and although what hair remained had turned silver, he covered it up with a baseball cap.

His hands reflected strength, the kind that comes from a life of hard work and hard play. Not a tall man, Hap stood at about 5-foot, 8-inches and his waist line had begun to reflect a few too many beers. Hap's plane, a 1956 single-engine Otter, was his baby. He called her Old Yeller, because of her bright yellow paint. About ten feet tall, and with a wing span of about forty feet, Old Yeller's payload capacity sometimes exceeded 1,700 pounds. In the summer season she sat on pontoons, and in the winter, skis. Old Yeller could land just about anywhere, summer or winter.

Having just dropped off some hardware supplies at a distant Indian settlement, Hap was done for the day and was anxious to land, get home, eat supper and go to bed.

The weather was pretty cloudy and stark. It was cool enough to keep a person from noticing it was July. But Hap knew the weather of northern Canada was nothing to count on. Often he would say, "In the north, you don't hope for anything, you just do the best you can."

Occasionally it would rain. Every twenty minutes or so, Hap would fly through a storm on his way back to the airport. Matter of fact, he was almost there, only thirty-odd air miles away, when he noticed the bears. His plane was in a gradual descent, only five-hundred feet above the ground, otherwise he never would have seen them. Also, there were five of them, which made them easy to spot.

From the air, the bears looked harmless. Five little balls of blackness pawing about. But Hap knew different. He suspected they were up to something.

The area where the bears were had recently been a site of controversy. You see, Hap was supposed to have picked up a canoeist there several weeks before. But the canoeist, who had been making a solo trip, had never showed. On the pickup day, Hap had waited for two hours, but the man never arrived. In fact, Hap went back for the next two days at the same time just in case the man was behind schedule. Still, he never came and the search had no result. Finally, the man had been given up for dead.

So Hap was paying more attention to the area than he would have under normal circumstances. He wondered about what had happened, and the fate that claimed the man's life. Thoughts about near-death escapes that he himself had experienced filled his mind. Like the time his propeller had fallen off while in flight, or when he had had to land on one ski. How lucky he had been!

Curious about what had the attention of five bears, Hap flew low to check it out. He saw that they were fighting but couldn't tell why, so he decided to land.

Upon landing, four of the bears ran away in the bush. One bear remained. As he taxied the plane toward the shore of the river, Hap could see the remaining bear was dragging a dead animal carcass of some sort. That must have been what the commotion was about.

His eyes fell to some brightly colored remnants of gear laying about the shore. The material appeared to be something like plastic or clothing. As he got closer, it looked more like cloth. It was. It was the clothing of the dead canoeist! The bears were fighting over the flesh of the dead man! Their teeth had torn the flesh from his bones.

Finally, Hap beached the plane and tied it off to a tree close to shore. The bear was still dragging the corpse and refused to leave it. After all, it was a free lunch. With no other choice, Hap got his .30.30 rifle from the plane and shot the bear straight through the skull. It fell dead next to what remained of the canoeist. Hap walked closer, his heart pounding from the excitement...and the grief.

All that remained of the canoeist was barely enough to fill a grocery sack. One thigh and half of a calf lay next to a partially eaten rib cage and shoulder blade. The skull remained but the face had been wholly devoured. All that Hap could guess was the man had drowned and his body washed ashore where the bears found it.

With a bandanna tied around his nose and mouth, to help dilute the smell of what remained, Hap gathered the leftovers. He placed them inside a stuff sack. Underneath what remained of the rib cage, Hap found one eyeball. He couldn't help but notice the man had had blue eyes. This discovery made Hap wonder if the man had been a blonde, like himself. He shuddered as he began to realize a connection with the dead man.

After he was finished, Hap put the stuff sack in the rear of the plane. He hoped the distance from the cockpit would alleviate the smell that poured from the sack. The smell of a dead, water-logged, half-eaten human body was nauseous; he also opened all the vents and windows in the plane so he could breathe more easily.

Within moments, Hap was airborne again and on his way back toward base. Finally, he landed, informed the appropriate authorities about what had happened, gave the stuff sack to the coroner, and went home. Hap skipped supper and went straight to bed, but couldn't sleep.

Laying in the darkness, Hap said to himself, "I knew I was supposed to pick the guy up, but that was ridiculous."

STORY OUTLINE

I.   A bush pilot is flying home from an Indian settlement when he passes an area where he was supposed to pick up a canoeist.

II.   The pilot notices five bears at the same site, wonders what the fuss is about, and stops to check it out.

III.   Upon landing, most of the bears run away – except one, which is dragging some sort of carcass. He recognizes the body as that of the canoeist.

IV.   The pilot shoots and kills the bear and picks up the remains of the canoeist. (Be as gross and graphic, yet realistic, as possible, when describing what body parts are left and how the pilot handles them.)

V.   The pilot puts the leftover body parts in a stuff sack and places the sack in the back of the plane.

VI.   Finally, the pilot arrives home and calls the necessary authorities. He thinks to himself, "I know I was supposed to pick the guy up, but that was ridiculous."

PART TWO

Stories For Every Campfire

The short story is the single most useful source for creating campfire stories. The stories in this section of the book include many classics, as well as stories told by Dave Scott and Scott Power and other original and wonderful tales.

Just a reminder: When you want to turn a memorable tale into a campfire story, the first step in the conversion process is to outline it. The second is to convert it to the third person. These conversions are important for credibility.

Anything that enhances the credibility of a campfire story is important. It will have more power, more of a dramatic effect.

You do not need someone in the woods acting as an accomplice, trying to scare the listeners. You can handle that perfectly well yourself with the simple telling of a good story line.

And remember, the story line must be thought-provoking.

That is the essence of a great campfire story experience. The listeners must ponder the events, must take the story with them – and as they snuggle into their sleeping bags, the story will magnify the natural events that surround them.

Enjoy…and don't let the bed bugs bite.

SCARED TO DEATH

By Scott E. Power

In a faraway land, but not too far, there was an old farmer. Through years of hard work and long days, he had become very strong and wise. In fact, he was regarded as the wisest person in the entire town. He was very proud of this fact. And he was vain enough that he never let anyone forget just how smart he was.

One day, while he was performing one of his many farming chores, ploughing the fields, he came upon a snake. It laid there in the dirt, motionless. The man wondered if it was dead. He questioned what kind of snake it was. It just laid there coiled up, appearing to be dead. The farmer couldn't stand his curiosity very long. He had to know if it was really dead or if it was just sleeping. Actually, the farmer had never seen a snake like it before. There were weird shapes on its back, kind of like the shapes in a spider's web. It seemed that it was an extraordinary snake.

The farmer bent over, stretching forth a stick to prod the snake, to see if it was alive. But after it was too late, he realized the foolhardiness of his behavior. For just as the tip of the stick was threatening to touch the snake, it sprang out of its coil as quick as lightening, bit the farmer, sinking its fangs deep into his flesh.

After releasing itself from the man's leg, the snake quickly slid away and coiled itself in the dirt. The shock and the horror of the bite was overwhelming for the farmer. He had seen snakes many times before, but had never ever been bitten. As he stood there in shock, wondering what to do, he realized that the nearest doctor was more than one day's journey away. Immediately, the man fell dead.

Many hours passed before anyone found the man. His wife was the first to happen upon him. When he didn't come to the house for lunch, she got worried and went searching.

Upon finding the dead man, she also saw the snake and killed it with the back side of a shovel. She couldn't help but kill the snake, knowing intuitively what it had done. She took vengeance, stabbing the snake with the shovel, cutting it into many pieces. She wanted to find out what kind of snake it was, since it was obviously poisonous. Picking up the bloody remnants of the dead snake, the wife wished she hadn't made such a mess. But she too had never seen such a deadly looking snake.

After having the snake identified, the farmers' wife was shocked to find the reptile was not a rare, lethal snake at all. It was just a common garden snake with unusual markings. The man did not die from poisonous venom. He had been struck dead by fear of a harmless strike of a common garden snake.

The moral of the story is to always be smart, but not too smart; scared, but not too scared.

STORY OUTLINE

I.   An old farmer is in the field doing chores.

II.   As he is working, he is bitten by a fierce-looking snake.

III.   Realizing the nearest doctor is one day's journey away, he falls dead.

IV.   His wife finds his dead body. Seeing the snake nearby she understands what happened and she kills the snake with a shovel.

V.   Later, she finds out the snake was not poisonous and that her husband died of fright.

VI.   The moral of the story is to always be smart, but not too smart; scared, but not too scared.

TATANKA SAPA AND HIS MEDICINE BOW

By David Scott

Daniel Hawthorne lived with his father Joseph and his mother Annette in a tiny one-room log cabin. It was a time when the West was still "wild" and when each step had to be taken with caution. Rumors of "savage" Indian tribes were known by all the squatters in the area, and the people said that if the Indians didn't get you, then the land certainly would. Because of his upbringing, Daniel believed those rumors through and through, even though his folks were generally good people who didn't spread falsehoods.

One day, while hunting, Daniel came upon an old Indian man laying helplessly in the forest. His first thought was to flee, until he saw how sick the old man really was. His fear quickly passed and he felt he had no choice other than to help him.

Daniel helped the old man to his feet, and although no words were spoken – at least none that were comprehended by either of the two – a great bonding had taken place. Slowly the Indian, with the help of his new friend, made his way through the forest carrying with him the last of all he possessed. The Indian kept on speaking in a language foreign to Daniel, and Daniel kept telling the old man how much trouble he was going to get into when he got home. On and on the two walked until finally they could both see the tiny log home. Upon seeing the cabin, the Indian seemed hesitant – almost afraid. Perhaps he had heard equally frightening stories of the "savage" settlers.

Daniel's parents were furious with him for bringing home an Indian. In fact, his father wanted to shoot the old man. Daniel ended the dispute by stepping between the two and reminding his father of the lessons which he'd learned.

"If someone is in trouble, no matter who they may be, you help them. Remember what you told me?" Daniel told his father. At that point, the reluctant parents had no choice other than to help the old Indian.

Over the course of the next four weeks, Daniel and the Indian become very close friends. He discovered that the old man's name was Tatanka Sapa, Black Bull. From his bed, Black Bull showed Daniel how to knapp arrowheads, set traps and play traditional Native American games. The two even learned words and sign language from each others language, but words did not need to be spoken for theirs was a friendship of the heart. As their friendship grew, however, the Indian continued to sicken.

Before the night of his death, Black Bull signaled for Daniel to come to his side. He reached beneath the bunk and pulled out a large bag made of animal skins, and motioned for Daniel to open it. Inside was the most beautiful bow, accompanied by ten meticulously made arrows. He gave the bow and arrows to Daniel and made the sign for brother, after which he passed away.

Several weeks went by, and one day Daniel fell asleep after finishing his chores. His mother and father were a half mile away gathering berries in the meadow. What they didn't know was that a grizzly bear was doing the same, keeping a careful eye on the couple at all times. The gnarled old bruin eventually became bored with the two, and headed toward the cabin. Annette sensed that something was wrong. No birds were singing, no animals were chatting, even the wind was still. At that moment she saw the large bear enter the partially opened door of the cabin.

She and her husband rushed with great speed to save their son, yet they knew they were too far away to get there in time. When they finally reached the front door, they were astounded. There, sprawled out on the floor before them, was the great grizzly bear. On the bunk beside the bear lay their son fast asleep.

No one could figure out how the bear had died, for there was no obvious wound. But when Daniel's father was butchering the great beast, he found a beautiful handcrafted arrowhead embedded deep in its heart.

Quickly he dashed into the cabin where Daniel kept the bow and arrows given to him by the old Indian. The arrowhead retrieved from the bear's heart was a perfect match with the arrows given to Daniel, and when he counted the arrows in the quiver, there were only nine. As for the tenth, it was gone.

STORY OUTLINE

I.   Daniel Hawthorne lived on the frontier at a time when Indians were considered dangerous enemies.

II.   He finds an ill, elderly Indian and brings him home to nurse him back to health, much to Daniel's parents' objections.

III.   The Indian returns Daniel's kindness with his friendship and a gift of a medicine bow. Then he dies.

IV.   Daniel is asleep in the cabin one day, when his parents see a grizzly bear break into the cabin.

V.   The frantic parents reach the cabin from their field, only to find the bear dead.

VI.   Upon butchering the bear, Daniel's father finds an arrow has killed the bear and one of the arrows has mysteriously disappeared from the old Indian's quiver while Daniel slept.

PIQUA

As Told By Scott E. Power

One hundred years ago, there was a man named Jonathan who worked for the railroad. His job was to bargain with land owners, primarily Indians, about the acquisition of the land needed to expand the railroad further west. His job was difficult and probably not worth the money. It was dangerous since people didn't like to give up land they loved. In reality, the landowners had little choice. The rich railroad owners, with their friends in government, would simply take the land if the rightful owners wouldn't give it up. It was unfair and unjust, but that's how it was done.

Word had spread amongst the natives that this sort of evil was happening. Other tribes had been "relocated" or simply killed off by mercenaries hired by the rich railroad owners. It was a no-win situation for the Indians.

Well, a certain tribe of Indians in what is now called Piqua, Ohio, decided they would fight for their land, even die if necessary, but would not give up their land to the railroad.

Word had reached the tribe that Jonathan would be coming to their camp to "bargain" with them for the land. The Indians knew the white man named Jonathan would make any promise necessary to get the land. And after the land was given over, the white man's promises would be broken like every time before. So the Indians would not give in. They would die first.

The Indians regarded the white man as evil. The white man called Jonathan was their enemy and like any other enemy must be destroyed. So the Indians devised a plan to capture Jonathan and destroy him. They understood that truly evil people would only die if their spirit was burnt from their body on a stake. So the Indians arranged a traditional, ritualistic ceremony to burn Jonathan, their enemy, on a ten-foot stake placed on the sacred mound altar to the gods. When an enemy was killed at the stake like this, the ceremony ended after the spirit fled from the burning body to the abyss of the cosmos, never to return.

It was very easy for the Indians to capture Jonathan. He was traveling alone and wasn't expecting any trouble. He didn't know how despised he was amongst the natives. He didn't know they knew the truth. He didn't realize his very presence was a threat to their lives and culture. He didn't know he was so vulnerable. He didn't know it was a trap. He didn't realize he must be destroyed.

The Indians tied Jonathan's feet together and pulled him behind a horse, dragging him across the ground, through sticker bushes, against rocks and tree trunks. By the time they reached the ceremonial altar, Jonathan was covered with cuts and blood and bruises. His right arm was broken and he was screaming in pain and terror to stop. STOP!

It was no use. The Indians would not stop. Jonathan was an enemy, a white man, a paleface, a liar, a threat to the survival and culture of all Indians. He was to die an enemy's death. A death of terror, torture, pain, misery and brutality.

By the time they had tied Jonathan to the stake he had lost consciousness. Once the fiery flames began to burn his flesh, Jonathan awoke to feel the pain. He screamed. AHHHHH!

Over the crackling of the flames, he could hear drums pounding and the cries of the Indians as they danced and cheered the death of their enemy.

Jonathan could feel life leaving him. He no longer felt the pain. Things were turning black.

The Indians could see Jonathan dying. Burning black on the stake. They could see his spirit pulling from the body. They cheered louder and yelled louder. The drums were pounding at a frenzied pace. The death of their enemy was at hand!

Suddenly, there was thunder and then all was silent. In the darkness, the Indians watched their enemy die as its spirit fled the cooked corpse. As the spirit left the body, the Indians heard it cry "Otah-He-Wagh-PE-Qua" (Translated: He is risen from the ashes.) Ever since then, the place where Jonathan died has been called Piqua.

He who works for evil eventually pays the price.

STORY OUTLINE

I.   A tribe of Indians in Ohio hear that the railroad will send an agent to try to talk them out of their land.

II.   The Indians realize that these deals are always broken and are only a method of stealing their land.

III.   The railroad land grabber is captured by Indians and burned at the stake.

IV.   Upon his death his spirit cries "Otah-he-wagh-pe-qua" – "He is risen from the ashes."

V.   Ever since then this place has been called Piqua.

THE LEGEND OF STIFFY GREEN

By the Reverend Mark M. Wilkins

Dogs, so the old proverb says, are man's best friend. While some might take issue with such conventional wisdom, for many others, dogs become more than mere pets – they become intimate friends and lifelong companions. And, if the tales told in the vicinity of Highland Lawn Cemetery in Terre Haute are to believed, at least one man has taken his relationship with his dog beyond life and into the realm of Indiana ghost lore.

According to legend, John Heinl was a well-known and well-beloved figure around Terre Haute in the early years of this century. An elderly gentleman without immediate family, Heinl spent much of his time taking long strolls through the town, his favorite pipe in hand, greeting and visiting his many friends throughout the growing area. Everyone, it seems, knew John Heinl, and the little dog that was the constant companion on his wanderings. Indeed, it seemed that the elderly gentleman was never seen in public without the company of his bulldog, Stiffy Green, walking protectively by his side.

Tradition suggests that the dog's unusual name came from the awkward gait of the animal, coupled with the fact that unlike most members of his breed, Stiffy was possessed of piercing green eyes. Indeed, new members of the community were sometimes startled when, stopping to speak to the affable Mr. Heinl, they found themselves under the close scrutiny of his small companion with the arresting green eyes. Stiffy Green was known to be fiercely protective of his master, never allowing strangers too close. It was even said that as John Heinl slept, Stiffy Green slumbered at the foot of his bed, guarding him in his sleep just as he did during the daylight hours.

In any case, the pair seemed inseparable, one never out of sight of the other. John lavished love and affection on his little dog, and Stiffy returned his affection by providing his master with company, comfort, and the companionship needed to ease the loneliness of his elderly years.

It was death that eventually parted the two boon companions. In 1920, the aged Mr. Heinl died in his sleep. While his passing caused much sadness among his many friends in the community, it was his dog Stiffy that was his chief mourner. The dog was inconsolable, refusing to leave his master's side even during his funeral and entombment in the family crypt at Highland Lawn Cemetery.

As the funeral service ended, several of Heinl's friends and distant relatives tried to leash the dog in order to lead it away to safety. At first, the dog kept his would-be rescuers away by snarling and showing his teeth. Even in death, it seems Stiffy refused to abandon his beloved master. Eventually, the dog was captured and taken to the home of one of John Heinl's distant relatives in Terre Haute. However, even in his new home Stiffy refused to be consoled.

Within a week the dog was reported missing. He was found shortly thereafter sitting mournfully by the door to the Heinl family mausoleum, patiently guarding the eternal sleep of his master. Again the dog was captured and returned to his new home, only to disappear once again. Over the next several months, this became routine. No matter how securely Stiffy Green was guarded or chained, eventually the little dog would escape the confines of his new home, only to be found several miles away, at the door to the Heinl family crypt.

In time, Stiffy Green's new masters gave up trying to keep the dog at home, and allowed him to take up residence in the cemetery grounds. At first, workers there tried to bring food and water to the solemn little animal, but these were refused with a snarl and a grimace from those flashing green eyes. For weeks, Stiffy Green sat nearly motionless at the entrance of the Heinl tomb, seeming to challenge anyone who sought to enter. Through rain and cold and darkness Stiffy Green stood resolutely at his post outside the grave, as loyal as ever to the master within.

And it was here that his body was eventually found. Time, weather and lack of nutrition had eventually taken their toll. As word of the dog's death spread, a number of John Heinl's old friends gathered to discuss what should be done with the animal's body. While some recommended that it should simply be discarded, others suggested that it would only be appropriate to allow the animal to be entombed next to his master and friend. A fund was established, and the body of the dog was transported to a local taxidermist, who stuffed the remains and transformed his corpse into the unnerving semblance of life. The dog was stuffed in the sitting position he had maintained for months outside the Heinl tomb. The eyes were left open, with brilliant green-glass orbs put in place of the real ones.

When the grisly job was completed, the body of Stiffy Green was placed inside the Heinl tomb, next to the crypt of the master he had served so long and so well. It seemed that his service to John Heinl was at last completed. But perhaps not quite completed. Several months after Stiffy Green took his place in the Heinl family mausoleum, a maintenance worker was leaving the cemetery grounds early one warm fall evening. Just as he was packing his car for the ride home, he heard the excited bark of a small dog coming from the direction of the Heinl family crypt. Since the presence of wild dogs was, of course, discouraged by the cemetery work force, he quickly decided to investigate.

As he neared the precincts of the Heinl mausoleum, the sound became clearer, and the frighten workman stopped in his tracks. Much to his horror, he realized that the sound he was hearing was a familiar one. He had heard it frequently, months before, in this very spot. It was the barking of Stiffy Green. Then, as suddenly as it had begun, the barking stopped.

Summoning all of his courage, the workman crept closer to the grave site and stared at the mausoleum through the line of trees that surrounded it. He heaved a relieved sigh. There was nothing unusual around the crypt. Deciding that this had been nothing more than the barking of a stray dog, or perhaps the product of his imagination, the workman turned and began to walk back toward his car.

Then something else caught his attention. Out of the corner of his eye he caught the movement of a figure, or a pair of figures, in the distance. He turned once again and stared with horrified fascination at what he saw. Through the dusk of early evening, he saw, walking quietly along the fence that separated Highland Lawn from the surrounding community, the figure of an elderly man smoking a pipe. By his side, there padded silently the figure of a small dog. All of this, of course, was enough to unnerve the unfortunate workman. But there was one further aspect to the scene that cause his blood to chill: even from a distance, he could clearly see that the dog's eyes sparkled bright green.

Since that fateful day in October of 1921, legend has it that many people in the vicinity of Highland Lawn Cemetery have reported hearing the barking of a dog coming from within the confines of the cemetery grounds at odd hours of the day and night. A few have even reported seeing the figure of an elderly man, walking on cool autumn evenings, strolling amidst the windswept leaves. While their descriptions of the figure do vary slightly, they all agree on one point; walking serenely by his side is the figure of a small bulldog with green eyes - eyes now peaceful and content, since dog and master have been reunited beyond death itself.

STORY OUTLINE

I.   The elderly John Heinl had a faithful bull-dog. The dog was named of Stiffy Green, due to its awkward gait and its piercing green eyes.

II.   The two were inseparable, until John Heinl died.

III.   The dog, Stiffy Green, refused to leave the crypt mausoleum no matter how people tried to remove him from the area.

IV.   The dog died of starvation and was stuffed and placed besides his master in the family crypt.

V.   A worker one night heard a dog barking and upon investigating, saw an old man and a dog, resembling John Heinl and Stiffy Green, going on an evening walk – an event that continues occasionally even to this day.

ONE CRUEL JOKE

By Scott E. Power

On a particular Friday night – no one is exactly sure when but many believe it was Friday the thirteenth – three boys were walking down a dusty road, amidst the fields and farms of northwestern Iowa. The road was very well known to the boys. Each had travelled it many times before. But on that night it was said that the moon hid behind the clouds like a veil, and the darkness was so thick that the road didn't look quite right.

As the boys walked, each one tried to scare the others with frightful stories. Each laughed with disbelief, except Joe. The other two boys could sense that Joe was somewhat scared by the stories and the dark road, so they decided to play a trick.

Soon the boys walked by the gate of the local cemetery. Anyone who had died since 1901, when the cemetery had been established, was put to rot there. Many tall tales had been told about the graveyard, some saying that on certain nights a person could hear the voices of the dead crying out for life.

As the boys stood in front of the fog-covered cemetery and glared into the entrance, the mist seemed to swallow the tombstones and crosses into itself. Joe began to tremble with fright. When the other boys saw how scared he was, they knew it was time to play the trick.

"Inside the cemetery is a grave that is so filled with evil that anyone who stands on the grave and stabs a knife in the ground will die," said Chris.

The third boy, Frank, continued the story. "Yeah, they say that if any-one stands on the grave, sticks a knife in the grave they will turn white as snow and die. I would try it, but I don't think I have enough courage. Are you brave enough, Chris?" asked Frank.

"No way!" exclaimed Chris. "I'm a coward. But I know someone who isn't a coward. Someone brave enough to even stick the knife in the grave. Someone who is too smart to believe such nonsense."

"Who?" asked Joe.

"You, silly! You're the bravest and smartest guy I know. Even Chris says that. Only you can do it. Chris and I are cowards," explained Frank.

Joe didn't know what to think. He never thought of himself as exceedingly brave. But he was flattered by the compliments from his friends. Actually, he was scared, really scared. But he couldn't let his friends down. They were important to him. But the thought of standing on an evil grave made him shake with fright. What if it was true? What if he did die? Joe didn't want to die.

In the distance the boys heard a owl hoot in the night.

"Well?" asked the other two boys.

"Well, what?" asked Joe.

"Are you brave enough to stand on the grave or are we wrong about you? Surely you're not a coward. Are you going to test the evil grave or aren't you? You can even use my knife to stick in the ground and prove that you were there," said Chris. "It has my name on it. It will show that you really had the courage to stand on that grave."

"O.K.," Joe answered.

Frank and Chris led Joe through the fog and up to the cemetery gate. Of course, there wasn't actually such a grave. But they knew of a grave with a really old, scary-looking tombstone. Joe was told to go to the old McDowell grave and stand on it – and to stick the knife into the grave to prove he had done it.

Approaching the cemetery with fictitious apprehension, the two boys stopped at the cemetery gate. "Here it is," whispered Frank.

"Boy, does it look bizarre. I would never be strong enough to do what you're going to do, Joe. For being just a kid, you're quite a man," Chris exclaimed.

"Well, are you going to stand there or go in? Or were we wrong about you?" threatened Frank.

Up until this point, Joe had been hoping that they wouldn't really want him to go through with it. His heart was beating fast, really fast. He didn't believe he would actually die, but how could he tell otherwise? Would there be such a legend if someone hadn't died while standing on the grave before? People wouldn't just make up something so horrible as a lie about an evil grave, would they?

Joe couldn't believe his friends thought of him as brave and strong. It made him feel good. But if he had known they were lying and playing a mean trick on him, he would have hated them. Joe hated being the sucker. They played jokes on him a lot, knowing he could be fooled easily. But they were his friends and the grave was a different thing. If they thought he would actually die, they wouldn't want him to do it anyway.

Joe said, "O.K., I'll do it. If you think I'm so brave, I guess I am. You guys know me pretty well. Besides, I don't believe the legend anyway."

As Joe walked through the gate Frank and Chris looked at each other and grinned. They knew what to do once Joe was standing on the grave.

Finally, Joe was standing on the edge of the grave, looking at the tombstone. Through the darkness and the fog, he could barely read the letters on the tombstone. It said, "Russell McDowell, 1854-1901, The first man buried in this cemetery, Rest in Peace."

Joe stood in fear all alone in the cemetery surrounded by the swirling mist of fog. As Joe lifted his right foot to step onto the grave, his heart was nearly pounding a hole through his chest. His palms were sweating and his stomach began to hurt. "I shouldn't be doing this," Joe thought to himself, "I'm not brave."

But it was too late. His honor was at stake. Aside from that, his right foot was on the grave now, and his left was following. Within seconds Joe was standing on the grave. His heart was still pounding like a hammer. He was proud of himself for taking the step. Now all he had to do was stab the knife into the ground.

At that moment, Joe raised the knife high above his head and with all his strength stabbed the knife blade into the ground. But because of his intense nervousness, he wasn't watching where he was sticking the blade and consequently stabbed the knife through the canvas on the running shoe of his left foot. Joe's only thought was to get off that grave and out of there as quickly as possible.

He tried to turn and run, but it seemed something in the grave had grabbed him by the foot and wouldn't let him go.

Chris and Frank waited a long time at the cemetery gate, hearing nothing. Finally they decided that Joe had played a trick on them and had gone out the back way, leaving them standing around like idiots in the cold night fog.

It was only the next day when they realized how their trick had backfired. The police came to arrest Chris, for they found his knife stuck through their dead friend's shoe on an old grave in the cemetery.

STORY OUTLINE

I.   Three boys are walking down a dirt road late one Friday night when they pass an old graveyard.

II.   Two of the boys know that Joe is quite gullible and decide to play a joke on him.

III. They tell him that inside the graveyard there is a grave so filled with evil that if a person stands on the grave he will die.

IV.   The boys tell Joe that they don't really believe it but are too cowardly to try it. The tell Joe that they think he is brave and strong enough to test the legend and suggest that he should.

V.   One of the boys even gives Joe his knife to use to prove that he stood on the grave.

VI.   Joe takes the knife and walks to the grave, where he finally gets enough courage to stand on the grave and plunge the knife into the ground.

VII. Joe tries to run but feels as though something from the grave has grabbed hold of his leg!

VIII. The other boys get tired of waiting for Joe, thinking that he left them there in the night fog by themselves as a joke on them.

IX.   The next day the police arrest Chris, for his knife was stuck in his dead friend's shoe in the cemetery.

BENEATH THE LONE POST

By David R. Scott

As a young boy, Brenton Fielding had always been fascinated with the lifestyles of Native Americans. Each day he would tromp through the fields near his home, combing the turned soil for arrowheads and artifacts. His room was cluttered with antique books, authentic clothing and other relics that he found in the woods.

In his later years he became less and less interested in Indians and began his career in agriculture. He enjoyed his life on the farm and enjoyed spending time in his fields tending crops. One day however, he found something that rekindled his love for Native Americans...a flint ax head. The ax still held its polished edge and became the farmer's most prized possession. He carved a beautiful handle for the blade and always carried it with him on his tractor when he worked.

One day, while reaping his autumn harvest, he accidently lost the treasured ax head. Brenton did not continue working, but instead began looking for the missing artifact. Much to his dismay, he could not find it anywhere, and he sadly returned to his home.

That night, Brenton dreamt that he was again a small boy coming home from school through the woods. Suddenly, an Indian appeared and began chasing him down the path in the direction of his home. The Indian's face was painted black, and his hair was tied in long braids down either side of his chest. Young Brenton ran faster than ever before, and with each step he could hear the Indian brave asking for his sacred ax to be returned. Brenton blasted through the front door, grabbed the ax and, out of fear, turned and killed the Indian with a blow to the head.

In his dream he dragged the Indian far out into the field so that no one would find his remains. He buried the body as deeply into the ground as he possibly could near a lone fence post.

A single crash of thunder awakened him from his nightmare. Brenton walked over to the window and gazed through the curtain of rain sprinkling over his crops. Due to the darkness he could see hardly anything at all, yet suddenly, a great flash of lightning ignited the sky, and in that one instant the only thing he saw was the lone fence post of his nightmare.

Days went by, and then weeks. The urge to dig beneath the post was overwhelming, yet the fear of what he might find there was even greater. Winter soon set in and along with the cold months came constant torment. All Brenton could do was peer out his window at the post swirled with a beard of frosty white snow. Everyday he hoped he would come across the ax head, to prove that the dream was a figment of his imagination, but it never appeared.

The breakup of winter and the blooming of spring was fast upon him. Brenton had nearly forgotten about the ax simply because he was preparing for the planting season. But while carrying a sack of seed to the barn, Brenton noticed the lone fence pole, and once more his torment returned. Running to the barn, he grabbed a spade and headed for the fence post.

Quickly he began digging into the soft muddy earth. His shovel was heavy and sweat poured from his brow, yet his pace was rhythmically steady. The spring mud slowly began piling up around his feet, and although tired he could not bring himself to slow down. Finally he heard a click.

He cleaned the remaining mud away with his hands only to discover the missing ax head embedded deeply into a human skull. Next to the skull lay a rotting wooden handle...it was the handle that he had carved.

Leaving the items where he found them, Brenton filled the hole and placed his best arrowhead on top of the grave. The next day the arrowhead was gone, and from that day forth Brenton never revealed the story of the lone post to anyone.

STORY OUTLINE

I.   A farmer finds an ax head, which he cherishes until the day he loses it in his field while working.

II.   He dreams that an Indian brave is chasing him, asking for the ax back. In the dream he kills the brave with the axe and buries them both in the field near a lone fence post.

III.   Thunder awakens him from his dream and in a lightning flash he sees a lone fence post on the property.

IV.   He resists the urge to dig beneath the fence post until the following spring.

V.   As he digs beside the fence post he finds the missing ax head, deeply embedded into a human skull, with the handle that he had carved for the ax rotting next to it.

VI.   He reburies the ax and skull and leaves his best arrowhead as an offering on top of the grave.

ICY FINGERS

As Told By Doc Forgey and Pat Sherwood

Editor's Note: This is a story which I came upon when traveling in southern California. It has been modified for campfire telling by Pat Sherwood, a Scoutmaster friend of mine.

Along the southern coast of California, nestled high in the rocky coastline, there was a great old stone mansion, where many years ago there lived a very wealthy and very wicked Spanish count. The house was grand, indeed, comprising four spacious floors, rooms that boasted high ceilings, beautifully ornate trim and large fireplaces. The magnificent hallways and banquet room were lined with exquisite tapestries, woodwork and paintings. The entrance was encased in a great stone facade that opened to a marble foyer with a large staircase. All of this grandeur centered around a giant patio. The west wall was completely constructed of glass and overlooked the ocean. The floor was tiled with large Spanish stone.

But this grand house has changed a great deal since the days of the count. It was taken over by a large conglomerate several years ago and converted into a business complex full of offices. The entire fourth floor is now rented and occupied by a Japanese firm. But it wasn't always that way. When they first converted the old mansion, there was a small American company renting that floor. As a matter of fact, it was still under construction when one of the American bookkeepers, a young woman by the name of Samantha Marie, actually met the spirit that for many years haunted the old building...the ghost of the Spanish count.

It seems that during this time of reconstruction, the second and third floors were still unoccupied. The bottom floor was vacant, except for some lumber, empty boxes, crates and barrels. It was this floor that led to the great patio. Legend had it that one night a duel was fought to the death by the wicked count and a famous Austrian prince. The count was supposedly killed, although his body was never found. It was assumed that the prince fled, never to be heard from again. No one really knows why the duel was fought. Some say it was over a beautiful Spanish lady with whom both were passionately in love; others say that it was because of a treasure the two had pilfered and which the count refused to share with his princely consort; and still others - the local Mexicans – just shrug their shoulders if asked, and say, "*Quien sabe?*"

Samantha's story started one day not long after her company moved into the complex. It seems that a young male clerk came bounding into her office one morning all excited and announced to the book-keeper that he had encountered the famous ghost the previous night.

The clerk's excitement and the suddenness of his appearance so shocked the bookkeeper that Samantha gasped and dropped her pen, splattering red ink all over her smock and, worse yet, on the ledger page that she had just added up. The page was ruined. Now she would have to redo it, all because of that idiot clerk!

"Now look what you've done!" she cried wrathfully, as she looked at the splotched work. "Will you just look at this mess, I wish you and your ghosts would get out of here!"

"I'm sorry Sam." the clerk said apologetically; "I'll fix it – it won't take a minute. But don't be mad at me, or I won't tell you about the ghost and you'll be sorry if you don't hear about it!"

"Then get on with it so I can finish up," she said. She was still upset, but the clerk was a nice kid and besides, he'd probably bug her to death until she agreed to listen to his story.

So, with all the excitement that can only come from youth, the young clerk started telling her how he had had to work late the previous night. He also told her that he and Jeff, another employee, were to meet in his office. After he'd finished, they were to go to town for some late night entertainment. But it seems that while the clerk was waiting patiently in his office, Jeff had his supper and then laid down to rest for a while. Unfortunately, Jeff forgot the engagement and slept on. He didn't wake up until after ten o'clock and, thinking that the clerk was no longer waiting, didn't come. Meanwhile the clerk had also fallen asleep and might have slept till dawn, except for the fact that the ghost woke him!

The clerk went on to tell her that the ghost awoke him by passing its frigid fingers over his face while groaning wildly. At first he wasn't sure just what it was. Then he felt the icy fingers again touch his face. When he heard the blood-curdling groans issuing from the darkness, he knew exactly what it was. He told her how he then remembered the story of the prince and the duel that was fought down on the patio. He was sure it was the ghost of the prince's victim, the ghost of the count. "You have no idea what it's like to have a ghost pat your face in total darkness," he told her.

"Pat nothing," she retorted indignantly. "You should be ashamed of yourself for telling such trash. And as for the count, everyone knows that he was supposed to have been killed downstairs and that they never found the body! And even if they had, they surely would have sent it back to Spain to be buried there. So why, then, should he come back here and into our offices just to pat your face?"

The clerk couldn't really say, he could only account that there must have been some unfinished business that brought the ghost back to the premises. And the clerk swore that he was telling the truth.

"Then just what did you do?" Samantha asked, with just a bit of sarcasm.

"I ran...I cleared out of the building in nothing flat!" answered the clerk, out of breath. "You remember how fast we got down the stairs during the November earthquake? Well, last night's run was more than just a run, it was a disappearance! I went down those four flights of stairs like a streak of blue lightning, with the ghost hot on my heels. At first, I thought it was actually going home with me, but as I passed the patio, it stopped."

The clerk went on to tell her how he was forced to stop and have a drink to calm his frazzled nerves so that he might sleep. Of course, Samantha did question him on the possible influence this drink might have had on his memory of the events he was relating. With this, the clerk left abruptly, with a vow that he would never bother to tell her anything again.

Not believing the least bit in ghosts, Samantha gave the matter no more thought. In fact, when you fall heir to a set of books that haven't been posted for nineteen days and you have to catch everything up, plus get your trial balances to work before you can leave for the Christmas holidays, you haven't time to think about ghosts or anything else, except entries. Even though she had been working fourteen hours a day for the last week, the noon hour of the 22nd of December, the day before she was to leave for the holidays, found the bookkeeper with a difference of $13.89. She had to locate the discrepancy and straighten it out before she could leave for home. She really looked forward to spending a week at home back in Indiana. Hopefully there would be plenty of snow. She really missed the snow. Well, no time for day-dreaming now, she had to find that lousy $13.89. That could only mean night work – nothing else would do. Her plans had all been made to leave on the eight o'clock train the next morning. So Samantha Marie would stay up all night if need be. She would get the books to balance and be done with it.

Samantha worked straight through until dinner, after which she returned to her books and settled down for work about seven o'clock. Her office was small, so she turned on all the lights to keep it from looking dismal and lonely. Books, ledgers and journals were piled up two feet high around her. If hard work would locate that nasty, hateful $13.89, then it would surely be found.

She had told the security guard downstairs on the ground floor to try and stay awake for awhile. For if she finished more quickly, she would soon come down and let him know when she was ready to leave. The security guard was in a small room shut off from the rest of the building, so sometimes it was rather difficult to get to him. He was the laziest and most sleepy person she'd ever seen. Although he was supposed to take care of the big building at night, patrolling it so as to keep away "vandals" and such, in reality the old man slept so soundly that a brass band, much less anything else, could not rouse him.

It was for this very reason that before starting her work, Samantha was careful to go around and check the locks and bolts herself, just to make sure everything was secure. She was sure that unless the vandals had keys or could pass through solid wood doors, everything was safe.

Samantha felt quite secure, with nary a thought of vandals, spirits, ghosts or anything beyond the $13.89. The bookkeeper worked, adding and re-adding and footing up. At last, about eleven o'clock, she had found the thirteen dollars and would have jumped for joy, if she had had the time. She wasn't out of the woods yet. The dollars were much easier to find than the cents. She must also find the eighty-nine cents before she could have the pleasure of celebrating.

So once again she went at the books. After much brain-racking, more adding and a great deal of prayerful thought, she at last had under her thumb another eighty cents. Eureka! Only nine cents out. She could get it all straightened out and still get some sleep. Inspired by the thought, she smothered her yawns, and again began to add. When she looked at her watch, it was ten minutes to twelve, perhaps she'd be able to finish before one. She worked on the nine cents for about twenty minutes before one of the cash entries looked to be in error. She compared it with the voucher. Yes, that was where the trouble lay!

"Finally!" she heard herself say, "Almost done!"

S-t-t! Out went the lights. There she sat gasping in astonishment...in total darkness. When from out of the pitch-black darkness, came the most horrible, blood-curdling groan imaginable. She sat paralyzed, not daring to breathe, doubting her own senses. Every muscle in her body was rigid with fear! Then it occurred to her, with some indigna-tion, that this just might be some sick joke of that silly clerk. Her fear turned to anger and she was just about to yell out at him, when sud-denly, she felt something long, thin and icy cold pass gently over her face. Her body stiffened. At first she was too afraid to move. She sensed now that this was no prank put on by some young clerk.

The icy touch continued to lightly caress her face. A chill as she had never felt climbed up her spine, forcing her head back, shaking her body with spasms. Never in her life had she been so afraid. The icy caress continued for some time before she realized that it felt as if someone with frozen fingers was touching her. Finally, she couldn't take anymore. She nervously tried to brush the icy, bony things away. But no matter how fast she brushed, the frigid fingers would only come back again. Her heart was pounding like a steam-hammer. Her breath came in gasps of deadly fear. Then, a bone-chilling draft blew, causing her once again to stiffen and not move. Again came that dreadful groan, long and labored, as if the someone or something was in intolerable pain. She was still too frightened to move or scream. The next groan seem to penetrate her entire being; so horrible was the groan that she could feel herself start to faint. She tried to move, to run, but only tumbled to the floor. And there, among her books and ledgers, Samantha passed into unconsciousness.

When she regained her senses, she was still in a heap among the ledgers. It was still dark and the cold fingers still caressed her face. She became thoroughly desperate. Her mind was racing. She had laughed at the poor clerk. Thought him foolish. Now she found herself in the same predicament. He would laugh his fool head off if he could see her now!

Suddenly the thought of the clerk laughing at her, finding something comical about her situation, just infuriated her. "No simpleton clerk, and certainly no ghost, will belittle me," she thought angrily and she scrambled to her feet. The fingers continued to stroke her face as her mind tried to rationalize what was happening. I must address him, she thought, but what in language? Did this specter understand English or Spanish, she wondered? Spanish would doubtless be more suitable, if indeed it was the ghost of the murdered count.

"Will you do me a favor, Senor Ghost?" she started out bravely and in her best Spanish. Her voice was trembling as she asked, "Could you tell me what it is you want? Is there something I can do for you? Because if not, I would like very much to be allowed to finish my work, which I can't do – if you'll excuse my abruptness – if I'm not left alone."

Surely being the ghost of a gentleman and a diplomat, he would take the hint and vanish. At least that's what the bookkeeper was hoping for. But maybe the ghost didn't understand her Spanish. At any rate there was no articulate reply; only another blood-curdling groan and again the icy fingers touched her face. Then there came such a mournful sigh, so mournful, that Samantha almost felt sorry for the poor thing. What could possibly be the matter with it? In her pity, all fear was lost for a moment. She asked the darkness that was all about her, "What is it that you wish of me? Can I help you in some way? I'm no longer afraid of you – let me help you!"

Then a strange thing happened, the fingers moved uncertainly for a moment. Suddenly, the ledgers fell with a loud crash and a cold hand took hold of hers, very gently. Samantha tried her best not to feel frightened, but it was very difficult. The cold invisible hand gently pulled on hers and she was led off blindly through the darkened offices. She could see nothing, not a glimmer of light showed, not a sound was heard, except her own footsteps and the faint sound of the invisible something that was leading her along. There were no more groans. For this she was thankful. She would surely have screamed and fainted, without a doubt. No sound, only the patter of footsteps and the cold hand that led her on and on.

The two of them, the icy fingers and her, traveled through the darkened hallways, through the great hall, then down the stairs to the second floor, then more stairs, going down flight after flight, until they reached the tiled floor of the great patio, close to the security office. The simpleton guard, she thought, was sleeping like a log no doubt, while she was being led about in total darkness by an invisible hand, with no one to save her! She would have yelled, of course, but she found it utterly impossible to speak or even move her tongue, that in itself being a bizarre and uncomfortable sensation.

But where were they going? Back into the unused lumber rooms that adjoined the patio? Nothing there except lumber, barrels and empty boxes. What could this ghost want of her? Then, in the middle of the room, they paused; the frigid fingers released hers, leaving her standing alone in the darkness. Samantha entertained the idea of running, screaming her lungs out for the security guard, but abandoned the idea when she found that her feet wouldn't move. As she stood there, shaking with fright, she could hear steps passing to and fro about the floor. She waited, cold and trembling. Finally the footsteps approached. Again the cold, chilling hand took hold of hers and she was led to the corner of the room. Obedient to the unseen will, she bent down and groped about the floor, guided by the cold fingers holding hers. Then she felt it, a cold metal object almost buried in stone. It felt something like a small ring set firmly in the floor. She pulled at it with all of her might, but it did not move. At this, she heard the ghost give a faint sigh and for a second the cold fingers pressed her hand, quite affectionately, then released her. She heard steps passing slowly onto the patio, and slowly fading away. Where was he going? What on earth did all this mean?

Samantha couldn't remember ever being so tired. She stood and tried to find the door in the total darkness. The clerk would have been revenged could he have seen her desperately fumbling at a barrel, thinking it was the door. At last, too fatigued and sleepy to continue, she dropped down on the cold stone floor and fell unconscious.

She must have slept for some hours, for when she woke the first light of dawn was beginning to creep through the window. She sat up and wondered if she had taken leave of her senses during the night. What on earth could she be doing here on the lumber room floor? Then, the images from the night before came racing back – she remembered! Half-unconscious, she crept about in the near darkness, seeking the small ring. There it was! She caught hold of it and jerked it hard. Nothing. She tried again pulling harder, suddenly she was thrown to the floor. It seemed to her as if the entire floor was giving way. There was a sliding, crashing sound and she found herself hanging on for dear life to a barrel that fortunately retained its equilibrium. Her feet were dangling in space. She turned her head to look. Down below was total darkness. She could not even see if there was a floor. Her fear turned to panic as she felt her grip slip and a chill suddenly came over her as she felt the long icy fingers from the night before wrap themselves slowly around her ankle. The chilling hand seemed to be guiding her foot to one side. Her foot came to rest on the rung of an iron ladder. Her first instinct was to get out, away from that pit, but the icy fingers pulled her back. After some hesitation, she took a couple of deep breaths to gather her courage and climbed down the ladder into the blackness of the pit.

It was damp and musty. The air thick and rancid. The floor seemed to be of stone. It was completely dark. Her fear was gaining control over her courage. What could the ghost want of her in this pit? That's when she felt the icy fingers again take her hand and begin to guide her through the darkness. Her hand came to rest on a large candle and was released. She searched her clothes in a panic, hoping she still had a match on her. She let out a sigh of relief when she found some in the pocket of her smock. Upon lighting the candle, she almost wished she hadn't, because next to her was a corpse, its mummified skin dusty with age, its mouth drawn back into an eternal scream.

"Could this be the remains of the count?" she thought to herself.

From behind her, she heard a low moan. Taking the candle and raising it, she saw another body lying in the corner between some old chests. As she slowly approached, she saw the skeleton had a long narrow sword resting in its chest. Beside the sword lay a medallion. Its gold chain still draped about the skeleton's neck, bearing a Spanish crest. Apparently, this was the remains of the count. But then who was the other skeleton, she asked herself?

The question was quickly forgotten. For upon raising the candle a little more, Samantha Marie took notice of some large and small chests that were arranged along the walls. Could it be the treasure? But, alas! Upon investigation, she found the larger chests proved empty. That wicked count! No wonder he couldn't rest. But upon further investigation, she found that the smaller chests were literally crammed with all sorts of things.

They contained big, heavy Spanish coins in gold and silver. Gold and silver dinner services with the crest of some unfortunate emperor still shined and glimmered inside. Magnificent pieces of jeweled armor and weapons were found next to beautiful jewelry and loose precious stones. Samantha was beside herself with excitement, but after some thought, she deliberately selected handfuls of the latter, giving preference to the diamonds and pearls, always having had a taste for them that she was never able to gratify! She packed them in a small wooden chest that she found. The gold and silver dinner services and armor were left, being rather cumbersome. As the sun rose and the new day began, the accountant climbed out of the pit, rejoicing with her chest of diamonds, pearls and other jewelry.

Needless to say, Samantha didn't go away for the holidays on the eight o'clock train. She did, however, go to the office and locate her missing nine cents, after which she unfolded the tale of the ghost and treasure to the authorities – only keeping quiet the matter of the wooden chest of loot. Historians theorized later that the Austrian prince murdered the count for trying to cheat him, and then became trapped in the secret vault, perhaps the trap door closed by accident. The count's remains, along with that of the prince, were shipped to their respective homelands for proper burial. Samantha hypothesized that the count's soul couldn't rest until his remains were buried in a manner befitting his status and had haunted the old building until this was done. For the ghost of the count was never seen again.

Samantha Marie never told of the box of jewels she kept, for which she was heartily thankful afterwards. For when the government analyzed the find, what do you suppose they offered her for going about with a ghost in the middle of the night and finding the treasure for them? Ten thousand dollars! When she refused, stating that she would take merely, as her reward, one of the gold dinner services, they objected. But the accountant finally had her way and to this very day they have no idea that she has all those beautiful jewels and lives very comfortably back in Indiana. Wouldn't they be furious if they knew? Of course, Samantha Marie won't tell. And now that you've heard this tale, I'm sure she hopes that you won't tell either.

To my knowledge, Samantha has related this story only to close friends and myself and when I asked if there was anything else she would like to add, she just smiled and said, "Thank you, count!"

STORY OUTLINE

I.   A grand stone mansion in Southern California, formerly the property of a notoriously wicked Spanish count, is converted into offices for modern use.

II.   Samantha Marie is told by a clerk how he had fallen asleep while working late one night and was awakened by the icy fingers of the count's ghost touching his face. She doesn't believe him.

III.   Being the firm's accountant, Samantha is working late one night to uncover a bookkeeping error. Suddenly, the lights go out and from within the darkness, Samantha feels the horrible icy fingers touch her face.

IV.   When she hears a moan from the ghost, it scares her so much that she passes out. Upon awakening, the icy fingers are stroking her face.

V.   Angry at how the clerk would be laughing at her predicament, Samantha decides to ask the ghost in Spanish what it is that it wants of her.

VI.   The icy fingers take her hand and lead her to the abandoned storeroom on the first floor, placing her hand on a steel ring that is buried in the floor.

VII.   Weakened, she is unable to tug the trap door open. Sighing, the ghost leaves her. Samantha, exhausted by the night's events, collapses by the door until dawn.

IX.	Awakening, she returns to the ring and tugs hard. Suddenly the trap door springs open, causing her to hang for her life above a pit.

X.	The icy fingers grab her leg and place her foot on a steel rung of a ladder that she then takes to the bottom of the hidden vault.

XI.	There she finds two skeletons – those of the count and a prince who had fought to the death over the treasure that she also uncovers.

XII.	Samantha takes the jewels and eventually the authorities allow her a gold dinner service as a reward, so that the accountant is able to live the rest of her life in luxury back home in Indiana.

THE BLEMISH

By Scott E. Power

Sarah stood outside the door, looking through the window. Inside the room, huddled in the corner, was Rick Reese, her doctor.

Rick stared outside the barricaded window. Beads of rain shimmered on the glass pane. From inside the asylum the world appeared separate, disjointed, as if it was another reality, another world. He could not believe what had happened. Gently, he stroked his cheek. He tried to forget it. But the memory was like a demon, always torturing him. Spiders would forever crawl upon his flesh. Life would never be the same.

Sarah opened the door and walked in. Her cheek was still covered with a small bandage. The wound was healing nicely. She didn't know what to say, but knew she should visit. It was, after all, her fault the doctor was vexed. It was hard to tell what ramifications something so ghastly might have on the mind of a person. Sarah didn't understand why she was sane. One month had passed since the operation.

The whole trauma was traceable to one night two months before. Sarah had been camping next to her favorite lake. She was with some friends and it was very common that they camped together. She loved to camp and the lake was very special to her. It was where her father used to take her as a little girl and teach her the names of birds and plants. After her dad had died, she said the lake made her feel close to him and help alleviate any loneliness.

The camping trip went very well. Everyone enjoyed themselves and were reluctant to return home and to work. But they did, vowing to return soon.

Sarah was washing her face one morning a couple of weeks after the trip, when she noticed a small, red, pimple-like bump on her right cheek. She was disgusted to see it. Normally, her skin was clear and smooth, but then again, nobody likes a zit. So, she put some ointment on the bump to help dissolve it.

After a week or so of treating the red bump with the ointment, it looked no better. In fact, it was even bigger, redder and looked like a boil. It was too gross to look upon and even hurt a bit. Without hesitation, Sarah picked up the phone and called her doctor, Rick Reese, to schedule an appointment. She would remove the pimple one way or another.

The next day she went to the doctor's office just in time for her appointment. She had to wait awhile in the lobby as Dr. Reese was running late. Finally, her name was called. She followed the nurse to examining Room B and waited for the doctor. When the doctor arrived he had her chart with him and was quite friendly as he entered the room. Sarah told him why she had come. He didn't waste any time examining the swollen, red bump on her face. The bump had grown to the size of a quarter and looked grotesque.

Within a minute the doctor made his diagnosis. It was an abscess. Sarah was relieved to find out exactly what it was. Dr. Reese prescribed some special medication and speculated that the abscess would clear up in about one week.

After leaving the doctor's office, Sarah went to the pharmacy and picked up her prescription. She immediately applied some to the sore. She thought about how relieved she would be after the disgusting cyst was all gone.

Religiously Sarah applied the medication, twice a day, just as the doctor had said – even more often when she felt anxious to have it gone. The sore was getting too much attention from people, who kept asking, "What happened to your face, Sarah?" Finally, she put a bandage over it to keep people from reminding her how gross it was.

After nine days had passed, Sarah had used all of the medication and the sore was still on her cheek. But now it was even bigger. It had grown to a width of two inches and sat on her cheek like a rubber ball. Even worse, it had blackened and was purple around the edges. When she touched it her whole head throbbed with pain. It even was causing her right eye to swell shut. She panicked and began to cry. Sarah was certain it was a cancerous tumor. Hastily, she got in her car and drove to her doctor's office. She knew she was supposed to make an appointment, but this was an emergency.

She entered the lobby and approached the front desk. By now her whole body seemed to be swollen with pain, like it would explode at any moment. Behind the front desk sat the nurse. When she looked up from the desk and saw Sarah's face, she gasped with horror. Immediately the nurse told Sarah to follow her. The nurse took Sarah to the room she knew Dr. Reese would request, examining Room A. It was there that the doctor performed minor surgery to remove stitches, boils and cysts. Sarah laid down on the examining table as the nurse went to summon the doctor.

Exactly one minute passed when Dr. Reese came into the room. Upon seeing Sarah's face he knew what had to be done. The abscess would have to be lanced and the tumor inside removed. He told Sarah what he was preparing to do. She asked if it would hurt. He said no, because he would numb the area first before removing the sore. Sarah asked if he thought it was cancer. The doctor answered honestly that he didn't know what it was and wouldn't until he had the laboratory test results. In reality, the doctor was worried. He had never seen any thing so absolutely hideous and disgusting in his whole career.

It took fifteen minutes for the numbing agent to take effect. Sarah was still awake and could talk to the doctor as he performed the procedure. After putting on sterile surgical rubber gloves, the doctor picked up the scalpel blade and positioned it in his hand for optimum control and a graceful cut. The blade was razor sharp. As soon as her face was numb, Sarah told the doctor to proceed. From that moment on, the doctor would forever regret the procedure.

The razor edge of the scalpel blade pressed firmly against the swollen black skin of Sarah's cheek. With an even piercing cut, the blade moved through her skin and across the tumor. As the length of the knife's cut grew and the edges of the laceration opened wide, crimson blood spewed forth and ran down Sarah's cheek. But at the same moment the cause of the tumor came pouring from the cut.

Over the crimson carpet of Sarah's blood came thousands of baby spiders, crawling from inside her face. For on that innocent camping trip with her friends just weeks before, a female spider had laid its eggs beneath the skin of Sarah's right cheek as she slept, with Sarah never knowing it. All over her face and all over Dr. Reese's hand the spiders crawled forth, looking for the life that their mother's care had promised.

Dr. Reese collapsed, vexed by the horror of tiny, creeping, crawling, spiders that the cut of his knife had given freedom. That night Sarah went home, but Dr. Reese went to the mental hospital in a straight-jacket.

STORY OUTLINE

I.   A woman is visiting her former doctor at a mental hospital for he has had a nervous breakdown and she feels responsible.

II.   The whole incident is traceable to a camping trip the woman, Sarah, went on a few weeks before.

III.   Soon after the camping trip, she develops a red pimple-like, bump on her cheek, for which the doctor prescribed some medication.

IV.   The bump gets much worse despite the medication, and she returns to the doctor for an emergency surgical removal of the cyst.

V.   He cuts the sore open, and out of the wound come thousands of baby spiders, crawling all over his hands and her face.

VI.   Sarah goes home, but the doctor is taken to a mental hospital in a straight-jacket.

THE NIGHT VISITOR AT LOCKWOOD INN

As Told By David R. Scott

Tucked away in the corner of a New England village sat the Lockwood Inn, an old stone mansion owned by the Blanchfords. The Blanchfords had inherited a vast expanse of wealth from their deceased relatives, and because the mid-1700s were a dark time overrun by pillaging thieves, the Blanchfords were extremely careful about whom they allowed to stay at their Inn.

One night, William Blanchford and his son Craig were playing an arduous game of chess, while Martha Blanchford busied herself with her knitting needles. Every now and then she would chuckle at her husband, who cursed as Craig continued to destroy him in their game.

Outside the wind whipped the tops of the trees, and could be heard howling down the cobblestone chimney and blowing the coals to a deep glowing red within the hearth. The rains pounded the roof top, and an occasional flash of lightning would illuminate the dimly lit den. Beatrice Whitfield, the inn's maid, who had served the Blanchfords for over 35 years, stirred the coals beneath the cast-iron tea kettle.

"A bit more tea, Mrs. Blanchford?" the maid pleasantly asked.

"Why yes, thank you, Beatrice," Martha Blanchford responded with a radiant smile. "It most certainly is a dreadful night, don't you think so?"

"Aye, that it is, ma'am. Pleases the soul to be within the confines of a warm and cheery den," the maid said as she filled Mrs. Blanchford's tea cup.

Just then a heavy knock came forth from the inn's massive oak doors.

All faces stared down the corridor. "Now, who do you suppose that could be out in this dreary weather?" Beatrice said, walking down the lamplit corridor.

"Best let me answer it, Beatrice. Something may be wrong." William Blanchford stated impatiently, angered that someone would interrupt his game of chess.

William held the oil lamp in one hand, and opened the door just a crack with the other. All that was visible outside was a long black cloak with the hood drawn loosely over the visitor's head. The drops of rain framed the hood with liquid beads, and the visitor's split leather boots were well-worn from travel. In one hand he clung to a knotted walking cane, and in the other was a small burlap sack.

"Please...please...I beg of you, sir. Share with me the warmth of your fire and tea. Have mercy on a pitiful old man who has nothing." The old man's voice stuttered and cracked as it came forth from his lips.

William stood silently without expression while the chilling winds filled the warm room. He had sympathy for the old man, yet he was still rather apprehensive about letting strangers into his home.

"Oh William, can't you see the old man is freezing? Let him in," Martha said over her husband's shoulder.

William opened the door.

"I'm sorry, old boy, but one can never be too sure anymore around here." William explained. "You do understand, don't you?"

"Aye, them bandits prowl on a night like tonight, yet all I ask for is a warm place by the fire, and a hot cup a' tea, then I shall be on my way," the old man said as he limped his way through the door. All eyes stared at the man's rather strange walk.

"Aye, 'tis proof that them scum roam the village on nights like this. One slit the back of me leg three months ago, and stole all I had," the old man solemnly said.

"Oh, you poor dear, sit down by the fire, and Beatrice will get you some tea," Martha said while helping the old man into a chair. Beatrice poured the old man a spot of tea, still not trusting his "good nature."

Soon the old man stopped shivering, and politely asked for another cup. Craig and William went off to their quarters, and Martha continued to pamper the visitor.

"Well Beatrice, I am off to bed. Sir, if there is anything you need, Beatrice will help you," Martha finally said.

"Thank you ma'am, you are too kind," the old man said with a sinister smile.

In a few short moments, Martha's echoing footsteps were swallowed by the drone of the storm, and the only audible sound remaining was that of the dry wood popping as it burned in the hearth.

"Well my dear, where is it that you sleep? Do you not have your own quarters in such a lofty abode?" the visitor asked inquisitively.

"Yes of course, but I shall sleep here on the settee in case you need my assistance...good night sir."

"Good night," the old man said with a disappointed tone.

Beatrice laid on the settee pretending to be asleep. She breathed in a deep rhythmic pattern, and left her eyes open only as slits. She did not trust the old man in the black cloak; something about him drew her suspicion. Perhaps she was being foolish. Maybe he was simply an old man with no place to go. Maybe he was telling the truth, and maybe he did simply need the comfort and care of loving people such as the Blanchfords.

However, after an hour, her instincts proved not to be fiction. The old man slowly turned and stared with cold eyes for a long time into the eyes of the maid. She managed not to break her rhythmic breathing, and kept her face expressionless. She watched as the old man stood from his resting place and moved across the room, never limping once. In the flickering firelight, he grabbed his small burlap sack and untied the twine that sealed its opening. Beatrice watched as the night visitor reached within the sack, and then she froze in terror.

The old man had pulled from the sack a severed human hand, and placed it on the wooden table near the stone hearth. Beatrice bit deep into her lower lip to prevent herself from screaming. She wanted to run and fetch Mr. Blanchford and his son, but she figured her best bet was to stay put. The old man retrieved a candle from the fireplace's mantel, and poured the hot wax into the palm of the hand. He then placed the candle in the wax to prevent it from tipping. Again, he looked deep into the face of the old maid, but she appeared to be fast asleep.

And then, he chanted in a whispering tone:

> *"Ancient hand from forest deep;*
> *Bring all within a soundless sleep.*
> *Grant them sleep throughout this night;*
> *To not awake till morning light.*
> *Allow your fingers to unfold;*
> *And point to me the Lockwood gold.*
> *In silence now I watch and stand;*
> *Now point, now point your hollow hand."*

Suddenly the fire flared, and a flash of blue lightning filled the tiny room, followed moments later by a deep crash of thunder. The candle's flame grew brighter within the open hand, and soon its fingers moved. The index finger pointed straight while the others slowly closed, and then the hand began to spin on the small oak table. It spun around the room twice, slowed, and pointed not toward the gold's hiding place, but directly at the maid. Beatrice bit again into her lip, till it was bleeding within her mouth, yet still she continued to breath rhythmically.

The old man seemed puzzled and repeated his chant. Beatrice could now clearly see the accents of his gaunt facial features in the flickering candlelight. His beady eyes were wide and wild with greed, and his teeth seemed to grind as he repeated the chant. His body was hunched over the candle and silhouetted by the fire, and his bony hands stretched skyward over the flames of the candle.

Again the somewhat withered hand spun around the table, only to slow and stop with its long wrinkled finger pointing in the direction of Beatrice. The night visitor slowly looked away from the candle at the maid, squinting from the blindness of staring too intensely into the steady flame. She did not break her rhythm, even though her heart was begging for oxygen.

The old man carefully picked up the hand, which still pointed at Beatrice, and slowly crossed the room toward where she lay. Using the candle within the palm of the hand as an added source of light, the night visitor crept toward the maid. Then, suddenly, he stopped when he heard a noise in the next room that startled him.

Quickly, he turned to see what had caused the noise, only to discover that it was the Blanchford's cat. Yet, when he turned the pointing hand away from Beatrice, he made another discovery – the outstretched index finger had folded and closed.

Slowly he turned and again faced the sleeping maid, and upon doing so, the index finger pointed at her once more. Her heart pounded and her mouth went dry. The old man slowly turned the hand away again, making an effort to watch both the hand and the maid as he did so. Sure enough, the finger closed, yet when he aimed the hand at the maid, it opened once more, pointing directly as the needle on a compass.

Certainly, if the old man realized that she was awake he would kill her, yet she remained motionless and watched as the old man drew nearer. A wry smile painted its way across his lips, and his steel black eyes twinkled in the flickering candlelight.

Soon he stood hunched over the old woman, staring at her with the intensity of a hungry falcon. The candlelight seemed to lick her face, and the only thing visible through her partially open eyes, was the long bony finger protruding from the hand on which the candle was perched. It was, of course, aiming directly between her eyes.

The old man continued to study her face. Certainly he knew that she was not asleep...was he merely playing a game with her, or was he genuinely deceived. The old woman did not know. He seemed to stare for an eternity, and then finally retreated to the table near the stone hearth. Slowly he placed the hand upon the oak table and again said his chant, the finger continued to point toward Beatrice Whitfield. She knew that she would eventually have no other alternative but to flee. Her mind raced and her heart beat wildly within the prison of her rib cage. The old man's eyes simply fell upon the maid, waiting for her to move, when at last she did. She exploded from the settee and ran up the massive staircase quickly as her legs would carry her. Behind she heard the night visitor coming after her, yet he wasn't running, he was merely walking, almost as though he knew he would capture her. Beatrice blasted the Blanchford's bedroom door nearly off its hinges, and shook both of them violently, but neither stirred. She screamed into their ears, but to no avail. She could hear the heavy footsteps echo throughout the long hollow corridor, yet still they were not running, simply walking.

She ran to another hallway that led back down some winding stairs. She was about to run out the front door when she glanced into the sitting room and noticed the hand pointing its gnarled finger and following her every step. Quickly, she cast the hand within the flames of the hearth, and headed for the door. The hand suddenly burst into flames with a violent explosion and the old man screamed in apparent pain. She heard a commotion upstairs as the Blanchfords suddenly awaken from the spell.

The old man fumbled with the front door and staggered through it into the blustery night outside, never to be seen again.

Beatrice was honored for her intuition and her bravery. It pays to not only have common sense, but the courage to back it up.

STORY OUTLINE

I.   An old man is let into an inn owned by a family called Blanchford on a stormy night long ago in New England.

II.   The housemaid, Beatrice, does not trust the old man and tells him that she will sleep in the main room with him "in case he needs anything."

III.   Beatrice fools the old man into thinking that she is asleep. He pulls a severed hand from a bag, placing a spell on the family to make them all sleep. Then he asks the hand to point out the inn's treasure. The hand points at Beatrice.

IV.   Beatrice sees her chance and runs for the owners' bedroom, but they are in a deep sleep.

V.   She grabs the severed hand and throws it into the fire, causing the old man much pain, allowing the Blanchfords to awaken, and thus saving herself and their fortune.

VI.   The moral of the story is: Use common sense and have the courage to back it up.

THE TELL-TALE HEART

By Edgar Allen Poe

True! – nervous – very, very dreadfully nervous I had been and am; but why will you say that I am mad? The disease had sharpened my senses – not destroyed – not dulled them. Above all was the sense of hearing acute. I heard all things in the heaven and in the earth. I heard many things in hell. How, then, am I mad? Hearken! and observe how healthily – how calmly I can tell you the whole story.

It is impossible to say how first the idea entered my brain; but once conceived, it haunted me day and night. Object there was none. Passion there was none. I loved the old man. He had never wronged me. He had never given me insult. For his gold I had no desire. I think it was his eye! Yes, it was this! One of his eyes resembled that of a vulture – a pale blue eye, with a film over it. Whenever it fell upon me, my blood ran cold; and so by degrees – very gradually – I made up my mind to take the life of the old man, and thus rid myself of the eye forever.

Now this is the point. You fancy me mad. Madmen know nothing. But you should have seen me. You should have seen how wisely I proceeded – with what caution – with what foresight – with what dissimulation I went to work! I was never kinder to the old man than during the whole week before I killed him. And every night, about midnight, I turned the latch of his door and opened it – oh, so gently! And then, when I had made an opening sufficient for my head, I put in a dark lantern, all closed, closed, so that no light shone out, and then I thrust in my head. Oh, you would have laughed to see how cunningly I thrust it in! I moved it slowly – very, very slowly, so that I might not disturb the old man's sleep. It took me an hour to place my whole head within the opening so far that I could see him as he lay upon his bed. Ha! – would a madman have been so wise as this? And then, when my head was well in the room, I undid the lantern cautiously – oh, so cautiously – cautiously (for the hinges creaked) – I undid it just so much that a single thin ray fell upon the vulture eye. And this I did for seven long nights – every night just at midnight – but I found the eye always closed; and so it was impossible to do the work; for it was not the old man who vexed me, but his Evil Eye. And every morning, when the day broke, I went boldly into the chamber, and spoke coura-geously to him, calling him by name in a hearty tone, and inquiring how he had passed the night. So you see he would have been a very profound old man, indeed, to suspect that every night, just at twelve, I looked in upon him while he slept.

Upon the eighth night I was more than usually cautious in opening the door. A watch's minute hand moves more quickly than did mine. Never before that night had I felt the extent of my own powers – of my sagacity. I could scarcely contain my feelings of triumph. To think that there I was, opening the deeds or thoughts. I fairly chuckled at the idea; and perhaps he heard me; for he moved on the bed suddenly, as if startled. Now you may think that I drew back – but no. His room was as black as pitch with the thick of darkness (for the shutters were close fastened, through fear of robbers), and so I knew that he could not see the opening of the door, and I kept pushing it on steadily, steadily.

I had my head in, and was about to open the lantern, when my thumb slipped upon the tin fastening, and the old man sprang up in the bed, crying out – "Who's there?"

I kept quite still and said nothing. For a whole hour I did not move a muscle, and in the meantime I did not hear him lie down. He was still sitting up in the bed listening – just as I have done, night after night, hearkening to the death watches in the wall.

Presently I heard a slight groan, and I knew it was the groan of mor-tal terror. It was not a groan of pain or of grief – oh, no! – it was the low stifled sound that arises from the bottom of the soul when over-charged with awe. I knew the sound well. Many a night, just at mid-night, when all the world slept, it has welled up from my own bosom, deepening, with its dreadful echo, the terrors that distracted me. I knew what the old man felt, and pitied him, although I chuckled at heart. I knew that he had been lying awake ever since the first slight noise, when he had turned in the bed. His fears had been ever since growing upon him. He had been trying to fancy them causeless, but could not. He had been saying to himself – "It is nothing but the wind in the chimney – it is only a mouse crossing the floor," or "It is merely a cricket which has made a single chirp." Yes, he has been trying to comfort himself with these suppositions; but he had found all in vain. All in vain; because Death, in approaching him, had stalked with his black shadow before him, and enveloped the victim. And it was the mournful influence of the unperceived shadow that caused him to feel – although he neither saw nor heard – to feel the presence of my head within the room.

When I had waited a long time, very patiently, without hearing him lie down, I resolved to open a little – a very, very little crevice in the lantern. So I opened it – you cannot imagine how stealthily, stealthily – until, at length, a single dim ray, like the thread of a spider, shot from out the crevice and full upon the vulture eye.

It was open – wide, wide open – and I grew furious as I gazed upon it. I saw it with perfect distinctness – all a dull blue, with a hideous veil over it that chilled the very marrow in my bones; but I could see nothing else of the old man's face or person, for I had directed the ray as if by instinct, precisely upon the damned spot.

And now have I not told you that what you mistake for madness is but over-acuteness of the senses? – now, I say, there came to my ear a low, dull quick sound, such as a watch makes when enveloped in cotton. I knew that sound well too. It was the beating of the old man's heart. It increased my fury, as the beating of a drum stimulates the soldier into courage.

But even yet I refrained and kept still. I scarcely breathed. I held the lantern motionless. How steadily I could maintain the ray upon the eye. Meantime the hellish tattoo of the heart increased. It grew quicker and quicker, and louder and louder every instant. The old man's terror must have been extreme! It grew louder, I say, louder every moment! – do you mark me well? I have told you that I am nervous: so I am. And now at the dead hour of the night, amid the dreadful silence of that old house, so strange a noise as this excited me to uncontrollable terror. Yet, for some minutes longer I refrained and stood still. But the beating grew louder, louder! I thought the heart must burst. And now a new anxiety seized me – the sound would be heard by a neighbor! The old man's hour had come! With a loud yell, I threw open the lantern and leaped into the room. He shrieked once – once only. In an instant I dragged him to the floor, and pulled the heavy bed over him. I then smiled gaily, to find the deed so far done. But, for many minutes, the heart beat on with a muffled sound. This, however, did not vex me; it would not be heard through the wall. At length it ceased. The old man was dead. I removed the bed and examined the corpse. Yes, he was stone, stone dead. I placed my hand upon the heart and held it there many minutes. There was no pulsation. He was stone dead. His eye would trouble me no more.

If still you think me mad, you will think so no longer when I describe the wise precautions I took for the concealment of the body. The night waned, and I worked hastily, but in silence. First of all I dismembered the corpse. I cut off the head and the arms and the legs.

I then took up three planks from the flooring of the chamber, and deposited all between the scantlings. I then replaced the boards so cleverly, so cunningly, that no human eye – not even his – could have detected anything wrong. There was nothing to wash out – no stain of any kind – no blood-spot whatever. I had been too wary for that. A tub had caught all – ha! ha!

When I had made an end of these labors, it was four o'clock – still dark as midnight. As the bell sounded the hour, there came a knocking at the street door. I went down to open it with a light heart – for what had I now to fear? There entered three men, who introduced themselves, with perfect suavity, as officers of the police. A shriek had been heard by a neighbor during the night; suspicion of foul play had been aroused; information had been lodged at the police office, and they (the officers) had been deputed to search the old gentleman.

I smiled – for what had I to fear? I bade the gentlemen welcome. The shriek, I said, was my own in a dream. The old man, I mentioned, was absent in the country. I took my visitors all over the house. I bade them search – search well. I led them, at length, to his chamber. I showed them his treasures, secure, undisturbed. In the enthusiasm of my confidence, I brought chairs into the room, and desired them here to rest from their fatigues, while I myself, in the wild audacity of my perfect triumph, placed my own seat upon the very spot beneath which reposed the corpse of the victim.

The officers were satisfied. My manner had convinced them. I was singularly at ease. They sat, and while I answered cheerily, they chatted familiar things. But, ere long, I felt myself getting pale and wished them gone. My head ached, and I fancied a ringing in my ears: but still they sat and still chatted. The ringing became more distinct – it continued and became more distinct: I talked more freely to get rid of the feeling: but it continued and gained definitiveness – until, at length, I found that the noise was not within my ears.

No doubt I now grew very pale – but I talked more fluently, and with a heightened voice. Yet the sound increased – and what could I do? It was a low, dull, quick sound – much such a sound as a watch makes when enveloped in cotton. I gasped for breath – and yet the officers heard it not. I talked more quickly – more vehemently; but the noise steadily increased. I arose and argued about trifles, in a high key and with violent gesticulations, but the noise steadily increased. Why would they not be gone? I paced the floor to and fro with heavy strides, as if excited to fury by the observation of the men – but the noise steadily increased. Oh God! what could I do? I foamed – I raved – I swore! I swung the chair upon which I had been sitting, and grated it upon the boards, but the noise arose over all and continually increased. It grew louder – louder – louder! And still the men chatted pleasantly, and smiled. Was it possible they heard not? Almighty God! – no, no! they heard! – They suspected! – They knew! – They were making a mockery of my horror! – this I thought and this I think. But any thing was better that this agony! Any thing was more tolerable than this derision! I could bear those hypocritical smiles no longer! I felt that I must scream or die! – and now – again! – listen! louder! louder! louder! louder! –

"Villains!" I shrieked, "dissemble no more! I admit the deed! – tear up the planks! – here, here! – it is the beating of his hideous heart!"

STORY OUTLINE

I.   A kind, old man has a blind eye, which becomes the object of obsession for his housekeeper.

II.   The housekeeper makes careful plans to kill the old man. He creeps into the gentleman's room each night to spy upon the old man and his "evil eye."

III.   One night, as the eye watches him, the housekeeper kills the old man. After he is dead, the housekeeper dismembers him and hides the body parts under the floor in the old man's bedroom.

IV.   The police arrive after he has cleaned up, saying that a neighbor heard a scream.

V.   He says he screamed during a nightmare, that the old man is away, and shows them through the house.

VI.   He sits with them in the old man's bedroom and places his chair over the floor where the dismembered body is buried.

VII.   While talking with the police, he hears a noise which he is convinced is the beating heart of the old man.

VIII. He talks as loud as he can, rants and raves, even eventually throws his chair - but the beating continues while the police smile at him.

IX. He finally gives up and shows them where the old man is buried.

THE CURSE OF THE SILVER SEAL

By David Scott

The old wooden boat sliced its way through the sea, plotting a course due south toward the lost ship Anna Marie. Jonathan Moore had been a treasure hunter for years and with some degree of success; in fact he had supported himself solely on his findings.

His hardy crew of five gazed without expression at the vast expanse of water that heaved before them. Their faces were windswept and their hands were callused, yet their souls remained undaunted, and their lust for loot drove them forth regardless of Jonathan Moore's stories.

You see, this was not Mr. Moore's first dive on the Anna Marie; he had been on this quest once before with his lifelong partner Thomas Hues. They too had that gleam in their eyes, that hunger for gold, that passion that makes man a slave of mammon. They too had ignored the legend and lore that surrounded the sunken ship in hopes of discovering a well-spring of riches. They had found the wreck and exposed a silver seal that stated that any man who dare venture near the ruins of the Anna Marie would either die or be forever cursed. When they dove a second time, only one came to the surface...and that was Jonathan. His partner's oxygen tank had somehow failed, leaving him prey to the merciless sea.

To that day Jonathan believed the drama to be an accident. His desire to strike it rich extended far beyond the curse of the silver seal. So, with his tiny crew, he looked out over the tossing mass of dark water, and dreamt of the Anna Marie. His movements mocked that of the vessel as it crossed the hills and valleys produced by the churning sea. The sun hung low in the western sky, dipping every now and then beneath a rolling wall of water, then returning to provide the final light of day. Tomorrow was to be the greatest day in the lives of the crew, the greatest...or the perhaps the last.

The wind beyond the cabin's walls pulsed throughout the night and the crew lay fast asleep. Jonathan remained awake however, pouring over maps, double-checking compass headings, and pacing the deck due to his excitement – or was it due to fear? Surely not. Jonathan reassured himself that what happened on his last trip was nothing more than a terrible accident. Finally, he decided that it was time to turn in, for the day ahead was to be a long and hopefully a bountiful one.

Jonathan was on his way back toward the ship's main cabin when something caught his eye. It was a figure standing near the oxygen tanks, yet Jonathan could not quite tell who it was. The wind picked up and licked his face, and he squinted from the salt spray that washed into his eyes. The figure was hunched over with its back to Jonathan and it appeared to be checking the pressure in the oxygen tanks. Jonathan waddled with the rocking boat toward the figure, attempting to pierce the darkness with his tear-swollen eyes.

"Bishop. . . Bishop, is that ... you?" he asked curiously, thinking it might be his first mate.

He moved closer still and repeated his question, the only response being the growl of the sea. Finally he stood above the person and placed his hand on the man's shoulder. "Bishop, why didn't you..." At that moment, the figure rapidly turned around and Jonathan staggered back. He was too afraid to speak, too terrified to move. The figure before him was a man who had long since been dead. It was a man that Jonathan knew well...the figure was none other than Thomas Hues himself.

His face was pale, preserved, yet washed white from lying beneath the sea for so many years, and his long wiry hair came to rest upon his bony chest dripping wet with salt water. His eyes were empty as the sea itself and his gaunt and bony body was hunched over. Thomas Hues' voice crackled as it came forth from his broken lips:

> *"A sunken ship 'neath stormy sea; a silver seal harken to thee.*
> *Taunting treasure fathoms down; with gold from lands of*
> *   Spanish crown.*
> *Ignore the lust within your soul; or pay old friend a heavy toll.*
> *Turn back turn back and loot no more; stand safe upon the*
> *   ocean shore.*
> *If not, old friend, then you must dwell; without a soul in*

ocean's hell.
A hollow body fathoms deep; a nightmare that is absent sleep.
Harken to the silver seal, or dine well on your final meal.
'Tis best to have an empty purse; because, old friend, the curse
is worse..."

The wasted man raised a gnarled, knotted finger and with a cast-iron, evil stare pointed to Jonathan. "...Because, old friend, the curse is worse..." he repeated. And with that he leapt over the side of the boat and allowed himself to be swallowed by the sea.

Jonathan stood holding his breath. He had heard stories of men hallucinating after spending too many days at sea, yet this seemed far too real. At last he managed to let out his breath, which stuttered as he did so. Slowly he walked over to the railing on the starboard bow and peered over its edge. Below the black water swirled over the hull of the boat, but as for Thomas Hues there remained no trace.

Jonathan slowly walked back to his quarters. Hallucination or not? What did Hues mean by what he said – "best to have an empty purse..." Jonathan thought aloud. What could that have possibly meant.

In his hammock, Jonathan gently swayed to the rhythm of the sea. Sleep, after that episode, was beyond impossible, and he constantly reassured himself that the entire ordeal was a mere figment of his rather unfaded imagination. Still, Jonathan lay in his hammock patiently awaiting the break of morning light. He stared aimlessly toward the ceiling of the cabin, pondering the past and praying for the future.

The thought of the Anna Marie nearly drove away all his fear. However, in the closet of his mind lurked the memories of the silver seal, not to mention the death and rather blurry resurrection of his "late" friend Thomas Hues. Jonathan, regardless of his fears, finally managed to fall into a spell of deep sleep.

The light from the morning sun stabbed its way through the tiny portholes of the boat. Jonathan, as he had always done in the past, got up, poured himself a steaming cup of coffee and stood on the upper deck. The wind cut through his hair and his boat cut through the icy water below.

Jonathan knew that he and his crew were nearing their mark...he could feel it. Closing in on a sunken ship caused the blood to boil in his veins, and the thought of the gold that lay below in the murky depth,caused his eyes to grow wild with greed. Yes, they were indeed closing in, and his crew was hungry.

At long last, the moment had arrived. The anchor was lowered and the engines were cut; below a fortune awaited. Final checks were made on the equipment, and each man suited up for the greatest of all hunts.

One by one the crew held their masks and rolled backward into the churning salt water. Their excitement had mounted to the point of hysteria, yet underwater, all was silent and serene.

Down the crew descended toward the ocean floor, spreading out in a rake formation as they dropped. Each man had a particular quadrant of sand to scrape, and each man felt certain that he would be the one to unveil the grandest prize. It was decided that the findings would be divided equally among the crew.

Jonathan drifted weightlessly away from the group. He had been there before and he never once forgot the hot spots of a site – he had a nose, a sixth sense for gold.

His feet tingled when they touched the sandy bottom. Deep inside his instincts told him exactly where to go, yet also deep inside he remembered the curse of the silver seal. His mouth went dry and his heart thumped. Perhaps he should have taken the seal's warning a bit more seriously, maybe a curse did in fact exist.

Above the rippling sea scattered beams of sunlight desperately attempted to reach the murky depths. Jonathan carried his fear like an uncomfortable pack, yet when he saw a gleaming object protruding from the sand, all fears melted away. Weightlessly, he bounded toward the object, with his greed and lust for gold stamping out all other emotions.

Even from a distance, Jonathan could see that the object was solid gold. Fish swirled about as he drew nearer, and his eagerness forced him impatiently along.

Before his feet, in the sand below, lay a Spanish cross, eight inches in length, six inches across, and three-quarters of an inch thick...solid gold. Its surface was embedded with rare jewels and polished pearls, and even though it was well over two-hundred years old, it still glistened in the broken beams of sunlight. The cross's value was immeasurable, and it was, without a doubt, the greatest find he had ever made.

Slowly Jonathan swam to the surface of the water, never once taking his eyes off the find. He did not even think to look for the other divers to show them his newly found prize – he simply ascended in a hypnotic trance to where the water met the sky.

The boat bobbed back and forth with a vacant deck. Jonathan pulled himself up the ladder clutching his golden cross. Quickly he removed his wetsuit and began meticulously cleaning the cross's surface. He paid no mind to the fact that the divers still remained beneath the sea, all he cared about, at that point in time, was the cross.

The jewels and the gold mingled in the sunlight and virtually blinded the eye with radiant brilliance. Jonathan continued to carefully clean and scrub the cross, and as he did so, he unmasked a small seal in its center...a solid silver seal. Of course, he immediately recognized the seal, for it was identical to the one that he had found before. Jonathan snapped out of his hypnotic state of mind and re-lived the warnings that were given to him.

His eyes panned the open sea, and then something strange happened. Jonathan raised the anchor, grabbed the spokes of the wheel and slowly turned the boat 180 degrees and aimed its wooden bow for the shores of home .

A crackled voice rang over the drone of the boat's motors, " 'Tis best to have an empty purse; because, old friend, the curse is worse..."

Jonathan throttled the boat to an even higher speed and focused only on the vast expanse of wealth he now held within his grasp, and never once did he look back. His crew perished in the icy seas above the Anna Marie.

Mr. Moore went on to receive the fame and fortune that he had long since lusted after. He explained to all who asked that his crew had been killed in a violent and sudden squall.

However, one night, while sitting alone by the fireplace in his mansion, something strange happened. On the mantel sat a beautiful conch shell that he had found when he was but a young boy. Due to his boredom, Jonathan picked up and fondled the shell, remembering how he used to place it to his ear in hopes of hearing the ocean. The old wives' tale made a thin smile cross his lips, and he placed the conch to his ear, yet when he did so the smile ran away from his face, and beads of sweat arose upon his forehead. He heard the ocean all right, but he also heard the moans and wails of his crew, whom he had left behind to die. The conch dropped to the marble floor and shattered, but the dreadful sounds of dying men and ocean swells, continued. Jonathan covered his ears, but the agonizing sounds only grew louder.

A raspy water-logged voice boomed within his brain, " 'Tis best to have an empty purse; because, old friend, the curse is worse...because, old friend, the curse is worse..." And then the voice broke into a horrible laughter that flooded the corridors of his mansion.

Quickly, Jonathan drove to where his boat was docked and headed through the open water toward the Anna Marie. Jonathan Moore was never to be seen again.

STORY OUTLINE

I.   Jonathan Moore is returning to find treasure lost at sea on the Anna Marie with a new crew of treasure hunters.

II.   His partner on the first trip, Thomas Hues, had died during their earlier dives for the Anna Marie's treasure.

III.   On the trip out to the site, Thomas Hues' ghost appears and warns his friend of the "Curse of the Silver Seal: " 'Tis best to have an empty purse; because, old friend, the curse is worse..."

IV.   While the crew is diving on the site, Jonathan dives off to one side and finds a large gold cross which he brings to the surface.

V.   He starts the motor and leaves the crew behind, to perish in the ocean.

VI.   He becomes wealthy from his treasure, but one day while listening to an old sea shell, he hears the moans of the drowned crew members.

VII.   He takes his boat back out toward the Anna Marie, never to be seen again.

THE MONKEY'S PAW

By W. W. Jacobs

Without, the night was cold and wet, but in the small parlor of Laburnum Villa the blinds were drawn and the fire burned brightly. Father and son were at chess; the former, who possessed ideas about the game involving radical changes, putting his king into such sharp and unnecessary perils that it even provoked comment from the white-haired old lady knitting placidly by the fire.

"Hark at the wind," said Mr. White, who, having seen a fatal mistake after it was too late, was
amiably desirous of preventing his son from seeing it.

"I'm listening," said the latter, grimly surveying the board as he stretched out his hand. "Check."

"I should hardly think that he'd come to-night," said his father, with his hand poised over the board.

"Mate," replied the son.

"That's the worst of living so far out," bawled Mr. White, with sudden and unlooked-for violence; "Of all the beastly, slushy, out-of-the way places to live in, this is the worst. Path's a bog, and the road's a torrent. I don't know what people are thinking about. I suppose because only two houses in the road are let, they think it doesn't matter."

"Never mind, dear," said his wife soothingly; "perhaps you'll win the next one."

Mr. White looked up sharply, just in time to intercept a knowing glance between mother and son. The words died away on his lips, and he hid a guilty grin in his thin grey beard.

"There he is," said Herbert White, as the gate banged to loudly and heavy footsteps came toward the door.

The old man rose with hospitable haste, and opening the door, was heard condoling with the new arrival. The new arrival also condoled with himself, so that Mrs. White said, "Tut tut!" and coughed gently as her husband entered the room, followed by a tall, burly man, beady of eye and rubicund of visage.

"Sergeant-Major Morris," he said, introducing him.

The sergeant-major shook hands, and taking the proffered seat by the fire, watched contentedly while his host got out whisky and tumblers and stood a small copper kettle on the fire.

At the third glass his eyes got brighter, and he began to talk; the little family circle regarding with eager interest this visitor from distant parts as he squared his broad shoulders in the chair, and spoke of wild scenes and doughty deeds; of wars and plagues, and strange peoples.

"Twenty-one years of it," said Mr. White, nodding at his wife and son. "When he went away he was a slip of a youth in the warehouse. Now look at him."

"He don't look to have taken much harm," said Mrs. White politely.

"I'd like to go to India myself," said the old man, "Just to look round a bit, you know."

"Better where you are," said the sergeant-major, shaking his head. He put down the empty glass, and sighing softly, shook it again.

"I should like to see those old temples and fakirs and jugglers," said the old man. "What was that you started telling me the other day about a monkey's paw or something, Morris?"

"Nothing," said the soldier hastily. "Leastways nothing worth hearing."

"Monkey's paw?" said Mrs. White curiously.

"Well, it's just a bit of what you might call magic, perhaps," said the sergeant-major off-handedly. His three listeners leaned forward eagerly. The visitor absent-mindedly put his empty glass to his lips and then set it down again. His host filled it for him.

"To look at," said the sergeant-major, fumbling in his pocket, "it's just an ordinary little paw, dried to a mummy."

He took something out of his pocket and proffered it. Mrs. White drew back with a grimace, but her son, taking it, examined it curiously.

"And what is there special about it?" inquired Mr. White as he took it from his son, and having examined it, placed it upon the table.

"It had a spell put on it by an old fakir," said the sergeant-major, "A very holy man. He wanted to show that fate ruled people's lives, and that those who interfered with it did so to their sorrow. He put a spell on it so that three separate men could each have three wishes from it."

His manner was so impressive that his hearers were conscious that their light laughter jarred somewhat.

"Well, why don't you have three, sir?" said Herbert White cleverly.

The soldier regarded him in the way that middle age is wont to regard presumptuous youth. "I have," he said quietly, and his blotchy face whitened.

"And did you really have the three wishes granted?" asked Mrs. White.

"I did," said the sergeant-major, and his glass tapped against his strong teeth.

"And has anybody else wished?" persisted the old lady.

"The first man had his three wishes. Yes." was the reply; "I don't know what the first two were, but the third was for death. That's how I got the paw."

His tones were so grave that a hush fell upon the group.

"If you've had your three wishes, it's no good to you now then, Morris," said the old man at last. "What do you keep it for?"

The soldier shook his head. "Fancy, I suppose," he said slowly. "I did have some idea of selling it, but I don't think I will. It has caused enough mischief already. Besides, people won't buy. They think it's a fairy tale, some of them; and those who do think anything of it want to try it first and pay me afterward."

"If you could have another three wishes," said the old man, eyeing him keenly, "would you have them?"

"I don't know," said the other. "I don't know."

He took the paw, and dangling it between his forefinger and thumb, suddenly threw it upon the fire. White, with a slight cry, stooped down and snatched it off.

"Better let it burn," said the soldier solemnly.

"If you don't want it, Morris," said the other, "give it to me."

"I won't," said his friend doggedly. "I threw it on the fire. If you keep it, don't blame me for what happens. Pitch it on the fire again like a sensible man."

The other shook his head and examined his new possession closely. "How do you do it?" he inquired.

"Hold it up in your right hand and with a loud voice, declare your wish," said the sergeant-major. "But I warn you of the consequences."

"Sounds like the *Arabian Nights*," said Mrs. White, as she rose and began to set the supper. "Don't you think you might wish for four pairs of hands for me?"

Her husband drew the talisman from his pocket, and then all three burst into laughter as the sergeant-major, with a look of alarm on his face, caught him by the arm.

"If you must wish," he said gruffly, "wish for something sensible."

Mr. White dropped it back in his pocket, and placing chairs, motioned his friend to the table. In the business of supper the talisman was partly forgotten, and afterward the three sat listening in an enthralled fashion to a second installment of the soldier's adventures in India.

"If the tale about the monkey's paw is not more truthful than those he has been telling us," said Herbert, as the door closed behind their guest, just in time to catch the last train, "we shan't make much out of it."

"Did you give him anything for it, father?" inquired Mrs. White, regarding her husband closely.

"A trifle," said he, coloring slightly. "He didn't want it, but I made him take it. And he pressed me again to throw it away."

"Likely," said Herbert, with pretended horror. "Why, we're going to be rich, and famous, and happy. Wish to be an emperor, father, to begin with; then you can't be henpecked."

He darted round the table, pursued by the maligned Mrs. White armed with an antimacassar. Mr. White took the paw from his pocket and eyed it dubiously. "I don't know what to wish for, and that's a fact," he said slowly. "It seems to me I've got all I want."

"If you only cleared the house, you'd be quite happy, wouldn't you!" said Herbert, with his hand on his shoulder. "Well, wish for two hundred pounds, then; that'll just do it."

His father, smiling shamefacedly at his own credulity, held up the talisman as his son, with a solemn face, somewhat marred by a wink at his mother, sat down at the piano and struck a few impressive chords.

"I wish for two hundred pounds," said the old man distinctly.

A fine crash from the piano greeted the words, interrupted by a shuddering cry from the old man. His wife and son ran toward him.

"It moved," he cried, with a glance of disgust at the object as it lay on the floor. "As I wished, it twisted in my hand like a snake."

"Well, I don't see the money," said his son, as he picked it up and placed it on the table, "And I bet I never shall."

"It must have been your fancy, father," said his wife, regarding him anxiously.

He shook his head. "Never mind, though; there's no harm done, but it gave me a shock all the same."

They sat down by the fire again while the two men finished their pipes. Outside, the wind was higher than ever, and the old man started nervously at the sound of a door banging upstairs. A silence unusual and depressing settled upon all three, which lasted until the old couple rose to retire for the night.

"I expect you'll find the cash tied up in a big bag in the middle of your bed," said Herbert, as he bade them good night, "And something horrible squatting up on top of the wardrobe watching you as you pocket your ill-gotten gains."

He sat alone in the darkness, gazing at the dying fire, and seeing faces in it. The last face was so horrible and so simian that he gazed at it in amazement. It got so vivid that, with a little uneasy laugh, he felt on the table for a glass containing a little water to throw over it. His hand grasped the monkey's paw, and with a little shiver he wiped his hand on his coat and went up to bed.

II

In the brightness of the wintry sun next morning as it streamed over the breakfast table he laughed at his fears. There was an air of prosaic wholesomeness about the room, which it had lacked on the previous night, and the dirty, shriveled little paw was pitched on the sideboard with a carelessness that betokened no great belief in its virtues.

"I suppose all old soldiers are the same," said Mrs. White. "The idea of our listening to such nonsense! How could wishes be granted in these days? And if they could, how could two hundred pounds hurt you, father?"

"Might drop on his head from the sky," said the frivolous Herbert.

"Morris said the things happened so naturally," said his father, "that you might if you so wished attribute it to coincidence."

"Well, don't break into the money before I come back," said Herbert as he rose from the table. "I'm afraid it'll turn you into a mean, avaricious man, and we shall have to disown you."

His mother laughed, and following him to the door, watched him down the road; and returning to the breakfast table, was very happy at the expense of her husband's credulity. All of which did not prevent her from scurrying to the door at the postman's knock, nor prevent her from referring somewhat shortly to retired sergeant-majors of bibulous habits when she found that the post brought a tailor's bill.

"Herbert will have some more of his funny remarks, I expect, when he comes home," she said, as they sat at dinner.

"I dare say," said Mr. White, pouring himself out some beer; "but for all that, the thing moved in my hand; that I'll swear to."

"You thought it did," said the old lady soothingly.

"I say it did," replied the other. "There was no thought about it; I had just – What's the matter?"

His wife made no reply. She was watching the mysterious movements of a man outside, who, peering in an undecided fashion at the house, appeared to be trying to make up his mind to enter. In mental connection with the two hundred pounds, she noticed that the stranger was well-dressed, and wore a silk hat of glossy newness. Three times he paused at the gate, and then walked on again. The fourth time he stood with his hand upon it, and then with sudden resolution flung it open and walked up the path. Mrs. White at the same moment placed her hands behind her, and hurriedly unfastening the strings of her apron, put that useful article of apparel beneath the cushion of her chair.

She brought the stranger, who seemed ill at ease, into the room. He gazed at her furtively, and listened in a preoccupied fashion as the old lady apologized for the appearance of the room, and her husband's coat, a garment which he usually reserved for the garden. She then waited as patiently as her sex would permit, for him to broach his business, but he was at first strangely silent.

"I – was asked to call," he said at last, and stooped and picked a piece of cotton from his trousers. "I come from Maw and Meggins."

The old lady started. "Is anything the matter?" she asked breathlessly. "Has anything happened to Herbert? What is it? What is it?"

Her husband interposed. "There, there, mother," he said hastily. "Sit down, and don't jump to conclusions. You've not brought bad news, I'm sure, sir;" and he eyed the other wistfully. "I'm sorry –" began the visitor.

"Is he hurt?" demanded the mother wildly.

The visitor bowed in assent. "Badly hurt," he said quietly, "But he is not in any pain."

"Oh, thank God!" said the old woman, clasping her hands. "Thank God for that! Thank —"

She broke off suddenly as the sinister meaning of the assurance dawned upon her, and she saw the awful confirmation of her fears in the other's averted face. She caught her breath, and turning to her slower-witted husband, laid her trembling old hand upon his. There was a long silence. "He was caught in the machinery," said the visitor at length in a low voice.

"Caught in the machinery," repeated Mr. White, in a dazed fashion. "Yes."

He sat staring blankly out at the window, and taking his wife's hand between his own, pressed it as he had been wont to do in their old courting days nearly forty years before "He was the only one left to us," he said, turning gently to the visitor. "It is hard." The other coughed, and rising, walked slowly to the window.

"The firm wished me to convey their sincere sympathy to you in your great loss," he said, without looking 'round. "I beg that you will understand I am only their servant and merely obeying orders."

There was no reply; the old woman's face was white, her eyes staring, and her breath inaudible; on the husband's face was a look of such as his friend the sergeant might have carried into his first action.

"I was to say that Maw and Meggins disclaim all responsibility," continued the other. "They admit no liability at all, but in consideration of your son's services, they wish to present you with a certain sum as compensation."

Mr. White dropped his wife's hand, and rising to his feet, gazed with a look of horror at his visitor. His dry lips shaped the words, "How much?"

"Two hundred pounds," was the answer.

Unconscious of his wife's shriek, the old man smiled faintly, put out his hands like a sightless man, and dropped, a senseless heap, to the floor.

III

In the huge new cemetery, some two miles distant, the old people buried their dead, and came back to the house steeped in shadow and silence. It was all over so quickly that at first they could hardly realize it, and remained in a state of expectation as though of something else to happen – something else which was to lighten this load, too heavy for old hearts to bear.

But the days passed, and expectation gave place to resignation – the hopeless resignation of the old, sometimes miscalled apathy. Sometimes they hardly exchanged a word, for now they had nothing to talk about, and their days were long to weariness.

It was about a week after that the old man, waking suddenly in the night, stretched out his hand and found himself alone. The room was in darkness, and the sound of subdued weeping came from the window. He raised himself in bed and listened.

"Come back," he said tenderly. "You will be cold."

"It is colder for my son," said the old woman, and wept afresh.

The sound of her sobs died away on his ears. The bed was warm, and his eyes heavy with sleep. He dozed fitfully, and then slept until a sudden wild cry from his wife awoke him with a start.

"The paw!" she cried wildly. "The monkey's paw!" He started up in alarm. "Where? Where is it? What's the matter?"

She came stumbling across the room toward him. "I want it," she said quietly. "You've not destroyed it?"

"It's in the parlor, on the bracket," he replied, marveling. "Why?"

She cried and laughed together, and bending over, kissed his cheek.

"I only just thought of it, " she said hysterically. "Why didn't I think of it before? Why didn't you think of it?"

"Think of what?" he questioned.

"The other two wishes," she replied rapidly. "We've only had one."

"Was not that enough?" he demanded fiercely.

"No," she cried triumphantly; "We'll have one more. Go down and get it quickly, and wish our boy alive again."

The man sat up in bed and flung the bedclothes from his quaking limbs. "Good God, you are mad!" he cried, aghast.

"Get it," she panted "Get it quickly, and wish – Oh, my boy, my boy!"

Her husband struck a match and lit the candle. "Get back to bed," he said unsteadily. "You don't know what you are saying."

"We had the first wish granted," said the old woman feverishly; "Why not the second?" "A coincidence," stammered the old man.

"Go and get it and wish," cried his wife, quivering with excitement.

The old man turned and regarded her, and his voice shook. "He has been dead ten days. and besides he – I would not tell you else, but – I could only recognize him by his clothing. If he was too terrible for you to see then, how now?"

"Bring him back," cried the old woman, and dragged him toward the door. "Do you think I fear the child I have nursed?"

He went down in the darkness, and felt his way to the parlor, and then to the mantelpiece. The talisman was in its place, and a horrible fear that the unspoken wish might bring his mutilated son before him ere he could escape from the room seized upon him, and he caught his breath as he found that he had lost the direction of the door. His brow cold with sweat, he felt his way round the table, and groped along the wall until he found himself in the small passage with the unwholesome thing in his hand.

Even his wife's face seemed changed as he entered the room. It was white and expectant, and to his fears seemed to have an unnatural look upon it. He was afraid of her.

"Wish!" she cried, in a strong voice.

"It is foolish and wicked," he faltered.

"Wish!" repeated his wife.

He raised his hand. "I wish my son alive again."

The talisman fell to the floor, and he regarded it fearfully. Then he sank trembling into a chair as the old woman, with burning eyes, walked to the window and raised the blind.

He sat until he was chilled with the cold, glancing occasionally at the figure of the old woman, peering through the window. The candle-end, which had burned below the rim of the china candlestick, was throwing pulsating shadows on the ceiling and walls, until, with a flicker larger than the rest, it expired. The old man, with an unspeakable sense of relief at the failure of the talisman, crept back to his bed, and a minute or two afterward the old woman came silently and apathetically beside him.

Neither spoke, but lay silently listening to the ticking of the clock. A stair creaked, and a squeaky mouse scurried noisily through the wall. The darkness was oppressive, and after lying for some time screwing up his courage, he took the box of matches, and striking one, went downstairs for a candle.

At the foot of the stairs the match went out, and he paused to strike another; and at the same moment a knock, so quiet and stealthy as to be scarcely audible, sounded on the front door.

The matches fell from his hand and spilled in the passage. He stood motionless, his breath suspended until the knock was repeated. Then he turned and fled swiftly back to his room, and closed the door behind him. A third knock sounded through the house.

"What's that?" cried the old woman, starting up.

"A rat," said the old man in shaking tones. "A rat. It passed me on the stairs."

His wife sat up in bed listening. A loud knock resounded through the house.

"It's Herbert!" she screamed. "It's Herbert!"

She ran to the door, but her husband was before her, and catching her by the arm, held her tightly.

"What are you going to do?" he whispered hoarsely.

"It's my boy; it's Herbert!" she cried, struggling mechanically. "I forgot it was two miles away. What are you holding me for? Let go. I must open the door."

"For God's sake don't let it in," cried the old man, trembling.

"You're afraid of your own son," she cried, struggling. "Let me go. I'm coming, Herbert; I'm coming."

There was another knock, and another. The old woman with a sudden wrench broke free and ran from the room.

Her husband followed to the landing, and called after her appealingly as she hurried downstairs. He heard the chain rattle back and the bottom bolt drawn slowly and stiffly from the socket. Then the old woman's voice strained and panting.

"The bolt," she cried loudly. "Come down. I can't reach it."

But her husband was on his hands and knees groping wildly on the floor in search of the paw. If he could only find it before the thing outside got in. A perfect fusillade of knocks reverberated through the house, and he heard the scraping of a chair as his wife put it down in the passage against the door. He heard the creaking of the bolt as it came slowly back, and at the same moment he found the monkey's paw, and frantically breathed his third and last wish.

The knocking ceased suddenly, although the echoes of it were still in the house. He heard the chair drawn back, and the door opened. A cold wind rushed up the staircase, and a long loud wail of disappointment and misery from his wife gave him courage to run down to her side, and then to the gate beyond. The street lamp flickering opposite shone on a quiet and deserted road.

STORY OUTLINE

I. The White family is at home on rainy evening when a former acquaintance, Sergeant Major Morris arrives.

II. He speaks of his travels and lets slip about a magical, dried monkey's paw that he has in his pocket.

III. A holy man in India had placed a spell on it to show that fate rules men's lives and those who interfered with it did so to their sorrow.

IV. The Sergeant-Major states that only three men can have three wishes. One man had taken his three - in fact his last wish was for death and that was when the Sergeant-Major got it.

V. The Sergeant-Major had taken his three, so there were no more remaining for him and, so saying, he tosses the paw into the fireplace.

VI. Mr. White recovers it from the fire, but the Sergeant-Major tells him he should let it burn.

VII. The Whites have everything they needed, but Mr White, at his son's suggestion, wishes for two hundred pounds, which would pay off their house.

VIII. After their son goes to work the next day, they notice a stranger who comes to their door. He announces that their son has been killed and that the company which he worked for has sent them as compensation two-hundred pounds.

IX.   The grief-stricken mother insists that her husband use his next wish to bring their son back from the dead.

X.   After he does so there is silence for awhile (the cemetery is two miles away). Suddenly there is a rapping on the door.

XI.   As his wife frantically tries to open the door, Mr. White finds the paw and makes his third and last wish.

XII.   The pounding suddenly stops and as the wife opens the door, there is only an empty road.

NOW YOU'VE READ VOL. 3 HOW ABOUT READING THE FIRST TWO IN THE SERIES

CAMPFIRE STORIES...THINGS THAT GO BUMP IN THE NIGHT
Book & Audio Tape by William W. Forgey, M.D.

Original and classic stories of adventure, ghosts, and all the things that you must worry about...the next time you hear something go bump in the night. Each story has been chosen to be especially easy to tell from memory. A large-print outline follows each story to assist in storytelling.

Listen to these original stories and adaptations from Dr. Forgey's two storytelling books, *Campfire Stories and Campfire Tales*. This tape, like the books, contains instructions on how to tell stories that will hold your audiences captive. Stories of mystery, adventure, ghoulies and long–leggety beasties.

Subject area: camping, fiction, storytelling

$11.95 paperback • $16.50 Canada • 176 pages • UPC code • 6x9 index • ISBN 0-934802-23-8
Audio Tape • $12.95 • $13.50 Canada • ISBN 1-57034-238-5

CAMPFIRE TALES... Ghoulies, Ghosties and Long-leggety Beasties.
by William W. Forgey, M.D.

Campfire Tales is filled with original and classic stories of adventure, ghosts, and other scary supernatural encounters. Chase ghoulies from a deep, dark grave; vindicate the misdeeds of a deranged madman; look over your shoulder for mysterious movements in the dark; travel in time to an Asian jungle; and discover swamps with eerie creatures from the night.

Campfire Tales is not just a collection of stories; it is a valuable resource for storytelling. Dr. Forgey discusses how to find and select a suitable story for telling around the fireside. A large-print outline follows each story to assist in story telling.

$11.95 paperback • $16.50 Canada • 176 pages • 6x9 • illustrations index • EAN /UPC codes • ISBN 0-934802-50-5

TRY SOURDOUGH COOKING WITH SCOTT POWER

COOKING THE SOURDOUGH WAY

Tips, Stoves, and Recipes. by Scott Power

Rise above ordinary food. Add zest to your baking at home or on the trail. Learn the lore and techniques of cooking with sourdough. And do it with style with this fascinating book by a young man who lived in a cabin for more than a year in northern Canada. Under these rustic conditions the author learned techniques that you will enjoy duplicating. Learn to make legendary sourdough pancakes over an open fire. Use your camp stove to bake sourdough breads. Bake sourdough biscuits in a dutch oven. Eat sourdough desserts. Pass your Sourdough starter down to family members as an heirloom.

About the author

Scott Power is a freelance writer and graphic artist who makes his base camp in Chicago, although you can rarely locate him there. Even though he is a cookbook writer, Scott confesses a preference to eat rather than cook. Scott holds a bachelor of Arts degree from Columbia College and is a member of the National Forensic League, Thespians, and the Wilderness Education Association.

$9.95 paperback • $13.50 Canada • 80 pages • 40 recipes • 6x9
ISBN 1-57034-008-0

TRY THESE GREAT BOOKS FOR YOUR SCOUTS

• •

COOKING THE DUTCH OVEN WAY Expanded 2nd Edition. by Woody Woodruff

$11.95 paperback • $16.50 Canada • 6x9 inches •176 pages drawings • EAN/UPC codes
ISBN 0-934802-51-3

The Basic Essentials of COOKING IN THE OUTDOORS by Cliff Jacobson

$5.99 paperback • $7.99 Canada • 72 pages • 6x9 • illustrations • index • EAN/UPC codes
ISBN 0-934802-46-7

The Basic Essentials of BACKPACKING by Harry Roberts
$5.99 paperback • $7.99 Canada • 72 pages • 6x9 • illustrations • index • EAN/UPC codes
ISBN 0-934802-44-0

An "Outdoor Life Book Club" selection.

The Basic Essentials of CAMPING by Cliff Jacobson

$5.99 paperback • $7.99 Canada 72 pages • 6x9 • illustrations • index • EAN/UPC codes
ISBN 0-934802-38-6

TRY THESE OTHER BOOKS BY DAVE SCOTT

PARADISE CREEK
A True Story of Adventure in the Canadian Wilderness.
by David Scott

Discover the joy and struggle of being cut-off from the "civilized world" while living in a cabin absent from modern conveniences. Bivouac at 60 below, hunt moose for winter meat, build a cabin and explore the far reaches of North Eastern Manitoba.

This is a coming of age story. The range of emotions stretch from the pain of frostbite and the fear experienced while lost for days in bitter cold temperatures to enjoying a cup of cabin coffee watching a summer sunset on a homemade swing.

About the Author:

David Scott has been interested in wilderness living since he first stepped into the woods. David is also a musician, song writer, poet, pilot, rustic furniture builder, and lecturer for such diverse groups as kindergarten to the Wilderness Medical Society.

$14.95 paperback • $19.95 Canada • 192 pages • 16 pages full color • 6 X 9 EAN/UPC codes • ISBN 1-57034-009-9

CAMPING'S LITTLE BOOK OF WISDOM by David Scott
379 Indispensable Bits of Camp Lore and Humor

This book was written as a reminder to all campers how special the backcountry is and how better to enjoy and appreciate it yourself. Here are some of the indispensable bits of camp lore and humor you'll find inside: 1) Wake up every now and then before the sun. 4.) "Minimal impact" means caring. 5.) Make an effort to carry no more than one third of your body weight. 6.) Stay put when lost. 13.) Wax or silicone your equipment zippers if you have difficulty in moving them.Do your best to enjoy the outdoors safely. 16.) See if you can follow an animal trail (proceed with caution if the tracks are larger than your own). 56) Never pack more than you can carry. 66.) Never tell your group you feel o.k. when really you don't. 67.) Remember that every pound on your feet equals five on your back. 104.) Store your water bottles upside down to prevent the lids from "ice locking" in cold temperatures.

$5.95 paperback • $7.99 Canada • 6x4 1/2 • 160 pages • EAN code ISBN 0-934802-96-3

The Basic Essentials of HYPOTHERMIA
by William W. Forgey, M.D.

Also known as "death by exposure," hypothermia is the lowering of the body's core temperature to a level of debilitation or death. It remains a top priority concern for all outdoor enthusiasts.

Distinguish between acute (immersion) and chronic (exhaustion) hypothermia. Prevent hypothermia by understanding its physiological effects and by adapting to conditions. Assess, re-warm and treat a hypothermic victim in the field. Discover the fatal effects of after drop and prevent disaster on your next excursion. Understand nutritional requirements, heat loss, the shivering response and insulation factors.

"The 72 page book is perhaps the clearest explanation of the subject yet."
—**Charlie Powell,** *Idahoian Daily News*

**$5.99 paperback • $7.99 Canada • 72 pages • 6x9 • illustrations • index
EAN/UPC codes • ISBN 0-934802-76-9**
An "Outdoor Life Book Club" selection.

DOCTOR'S LITTLE BOOK OF WISDOM
by William W. Forgey, M.D.

Tips gathered from the personal experiences of a successful physician over the past twenty years. In short and sweet sentences remember important practices to prevent disease and accidents that doctors commonly treat. The ounce of prevention that will provide a ton of cure.

About the author:
Dr. Forgey is a Clinical Assistant Professor of Family Medicine at Indiana University School of Medicine, a Board Member of the International Association of Medical Assistance for Travelers, the Wilderness Medical Society, and the Wilderness Education Association. He is the author of 14 books and multiple magazine articles dealing with health care issues.

**$5.95 paperback • $7.95 Canada • 6 x 4 1/2
160 pages • ISBN 1-57034-016-1**